ARCHBISHOP GREEN
His Life and Opinions

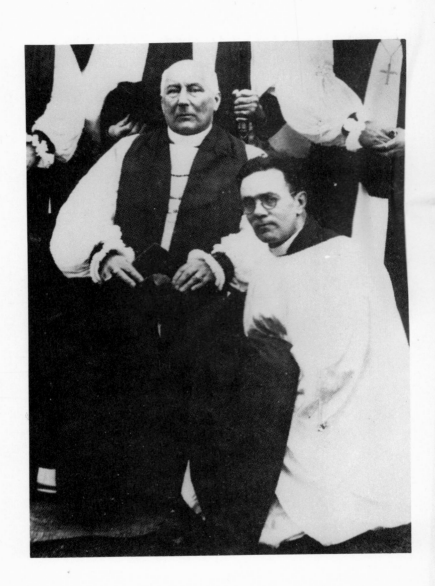

ARCHBISHOP GREEN

His Life and Opinions

A. J. EDWARDS

Best wishes,
Arthur.

GOMER

First Impression—September 1986

ISBN 0 86383 254 7

© A. J. Edwards

Printed at Gomer Press, Llandysul, Dyfed.

CONTENTS

Preface

Biographies of archbishops do not figure prominently on the reading-lists of history students. Yet their lives, like those of many other professional people, may affect the societies in which they live as much as the behaviour of politicians who never lack biographies. Certainly no student of the Church in modern Wales should ignore the subject of this biography. Nor should any student of the history of modern Wales ignore the disestablishment and disendowment of the Church in Wales. This biography seeks to deepen our understanding of the arguments in the disestablishment campaign that have been seen all too often from only one side. It is hoped that the enthusiasm for local history in Wales will be encouraged by the contribution of this biography to our understanding of the communities in which Green lived and to the way in which their preoccupations illuminate the central issues of the day.

This book has been written in my limited leisure-time during the last ten years. I was encouraged to write it by the response that I received to my article, *Bishop Green of Monmouth*, in the Journal of the Historical Society of the Church in Wales in 1971. I am grateful to the editor of that journal for allowing me to use material from my article in chapters four and five. I should like to record my debt to Canon E.T. Davies and to Chancellor O.G. Rees for encouragement and to Archdeacon Wallis Thomas for lending me the few letters that he managed to salvage from the Hon. Mrs. Green's bonfire of the private papers after Green's death. All Green's other letters are deposited in St. Deiniol's Library, Hawarden and his diaries are housed at the National Library of Wales, Aberystwyth. I am indebted to the successive librarians and their staffs and also to the Central Libraries at Cardiff and Aberdare for their co-operation over the past ten years. I am grateful to Mr. W.R. Jones, the former Secretary of the Representative Body, for allowing me to consult the copies of the Minutes of the Governing Body at 39 Cathedral Road. The Revd Canon C.W. Arthur, former Vicar of Aberdare, kindly showed me the consuetudinary and directory for the Vicar of Aberdare, which Green had compiled, as well as past numbers of the Aberdare Parish Magazine. One of Green's nephews, the late Mr. J.C.P. de Winton, kindly showed me the family scrapbooks that were loaned to him by the dowager Lady Merthyr.

Mr. Alan Davies, M.Sc., a former colleague at the Bishop of Llandaff School, assisted my limited knowledge of Welsh by translating certain passages. Archdeacon Owain Jones read the first draft of my manuscript and saved me from several errors. The defects that remain are entirely my own work.

Griffithstown, Pontypool.

A. J. Edwards

1. In the beginning

"I often think it's comical-Fal, lal, la!
How Nature always does contrive-Fal, lal, la!
That every boy and every gal
That's born into the world alive
Is either a little Liberal
Or else a little Conservative!"

Charles Alfred Howell Green was born on 19th August, 1864. The decade in which he was born began with the death of Prince Albert and ended with the Education Act. In this decade the privileged security of the old middle class began to pass away and a new age was born and nurtured by the parliamentary legislation of the two succeeding decades. In 1864 Palmerston was still Prime Minister, but he was eighty years old and he was more conservative than the Tories.

Green was born in the Diocese of St. David's which was to be his home for the next eighteen years. Connop Thirlwall had been the bishop of this vast diocese since 1840 when he had been rescued by Lord Melbourne from his scholarly pursuits in a Yorkshire country rectory as a reward for his liberal ideas. By 1864 Thirlwall, like Palmerston, was out of step with the new liberalism.

In the Church of England, to whose province of Canterbury the Diocese of St. David's belonged in 1864, the new liberalism was represented by a book of essays called *Essays and Reviews*. Thirlwall had not attended the session of Convocation that had condemned the book, but he joined his fellow-bishops in failing to understand how clergymen who had subscribed the Thirty-nine Articles of the Church of England could engage in such Biblical criticism. Of more immediate concern to Thirlwall was the contribution to the book of essays by Rowland Williams, the vice-principal of St. David's College, Lampeter, which was in Thirlwall's diocese and was awaiting authority to grant its own B.A. degree. Williams resigned from Lampeter and retired to a country parish in Wiltshire.

Green was born in the parish of Llanelli not far from the famous Stradey Park, though Rugby football had not arrived in Llanelli when Elizabeth Green, the wife of the senior assistant curate, Alfred John Morgan Green, gave birth to her first child. Elizabeth was the daughter of Richard Thomas Howell, a well-known local merchant. Her maternal grandfather was the Vicar of Llanelli and it was not therefore very surprising that she should have married the curate upon whom her grandfather, Ebenezer Morris, had come to rely so heavily in his old age. At the time of her wedding, eleven months before Charles Green's birth, Elizabeth was twenty-one and Alfred was thirty.

Both Elizabeth and Alfred had grown up in the privileged security of the middle class. It could in fact be argued that Alfred Green belonged to the class of lesser gentry or squires because he had been brought up on the Court Henry Estate in Carmarthenshire which his father, George Wade Green, a clergyman, had bought in 1830 with the help of money that he had inherited from his own father, Francis Green, a London clockmaker. George Green built an estate church at Court Henry for his family and tenants, but he never held a parish in the Diocese of St. David's. Alfred John Morgan Green was his eleventh child and the third of his sons to take Holy Orders. He was ordained by Bishop Connop Thirlwall in 1857.

Alfred Green's significant contribution to the improvement of the worship at Llanelli parish church has been recorded for posterity.[1] Ebenezer Morris, the incumbent since 1820, was an old man in failing health, but it was through him that Charles Green would one day be able to claim that he was descended from Peter Williams, the eighteenth century Methodist leader, whose grand-daughter had married Ebenezer Morris just as Morris's grand-daughter had married Alfred Green.

In 1864 Llanelli was a prosperous town of some importance in the industrial development of South Wales particularly through the manufacture of tinplate. The population of 3,000 in 1801 had increased to 17,000 by the time of Green's birth and would almost double itself by the end of the century. With the influx of industrial labour to the town chapels had proliferated. Politically a Liberal stronghold, Llanelli returned a Liberal M.P. unopposed in 1864 as it had on previous occasions.

The immigration of labour had made it necessary to build new houses and Llanelli had a good reputation for house-building in the nineteenth century. So the New Road in which Charles Green was born was thirty-five years old when he arrived, but it was not at all the kind of makeshift accommodation that is often associated with that stage of the Industrial Revolution. New Road consisted of solid middle-class town houses appropriate for the birth of this scion of a prosperous Victorian middle class family.

Born in one expanding industrial town, Charles Green was later to spend nearly half of his long ministry in the industrial parish of Aberdare, but Green knew little of Llanelli in his childhood because the death of old Ebenezer Morris in 1867 brought a new pharaoh to Llanelli vicarage who knew not Alfred John, and Green's father was transferred to the post of Master of the Cathedral School at St. David's where he had himself once been a pupil. This was attached to a minor canonry at the cathedral. With his brother Kenneth who had been born in May 1866, Charles Green and his parents left Llanelli for St. David's in July 1867.

St. David's 1867-74

St. David's was a far cry from industrial Llanelli because the Cathedral city was only a small village sixteen miles from the nearest railway station. Its location in proximity to the sea since its association with the Celtic saints, made St. David's more accessible to the Church of Ireland than it was to the parishes of Radnorshire of which it was the mother church.

In the years after 1860 many cathedrals came to terms with their isolation from the life of their dioceses by restoring their fabric and reviving their worship. The problem was exacerbated at St. David's by its geographical remoteness so that the Bishop, the Dean, the four Archdeacons of the diocese and most of the cathedral chapter lived elsewhere. The Bishop was at Abergwili Palace near Carmarthen; the Dean was at Lampeter where he was the principal of St. David's College, and the archdeacons were also pluralists, one being Professor of Latin at Lampeter and another headmaster of Carmarthen Grammar School. For much of the time that Alfred Green was in charge of the Cathedral School and Bishop's Vicar at the Cathedral he was left to conduct many of the services himself.

While the Green family was at St. David's the cathedral was being restored at the hands of Gilbert Scott who was reinstating the medieval design on the west front of the cathedral after the work that had been carried out there by Nash at the end of the eighteenth century. Here Charles Green received his first childhood impressions of the public worship of the Church. Throughout his life he supported the removal of eighteenth-century bad-taste in favour of medieval splendour.

Until the eve of his tenth birthday Charles Green received his elementary education at the hands of his own father in the small Cathedral Grammar School at St. David's. In 1869 there were ten day-boys and eleven boarders at the school which taught Classics, Mathematics, Divinity and English, and Welsh "if there was no objection to it"![2] That Green's primary education was so thorough is a tribute to his father for whom he retained a profound respect throughout his life, but the isolation of his early upbringing accounts for two features in Green's character, the one his loyalty and devotion to his family with whom he retained the closest contacts throughout his life; the other the natural reserve and shyness that was often misunderstood in later life. In the early days at St. David's his brother, Kenneth, two years younger but able to keep up with his brother's games, seems to have been Charles Green's only play-mate.

The family was a very close one and the period spent at St. David's was one of great happiness for them. Within two years of their arrival there, Charles and Kenneth found that they had both a brother and a sister. Sebert, the third child, was one day to become a physician to King George V. Elswith, known as Elsie in the family, was born in July

1869. Two other sons were born before the Green family left St. David's; Eric, who was killed in India in 1900 while an officer in the Royal Engineers, and Wilfrith who served as an officer in France during the first world war.

The happy days at St. David's where Charles Green first learned to ride a pony after receiving one for his fifth birthday, came to an end through no initiative of Alfred Green's but simply through the retirement of Bishop Connop Thirlwall to Bath on the grounds of ill-health in 1874. If the Bishop went, then his Vicar should go too, but provision was made for Alfred Green through his institution and induction to the living of Warren with St. Twynnell in south Pembrokeshire in the gift of the Dean and Chapter of St. David's. Here the family moved at the end of July 1874 when the Cathedral School said farewell to another, almost the last, in its long line of masters since the reign of Elizabeth 1.

Warren Vicarage 1874-78

Churchgoers in the Diocese of St. David's remembered 1874 as the year when their English Bishop, whose Welsh they did not understand, resigned and was succeeded by a Bishop named Jones whose Welsh was not much better. Students of Church History remember 1874 as the year of the passing of the Public Worship Regulation Act which tried to regulate the ritualism in the Church of England that had become a feature of the second stage of the Oxford Movement. Ritualism, as ceremonialism was popularly called, had its supporters in Wales and we shall return to that later, but there was little trace of it in the remote south Pembrokeshire parish of Warren in 1874 and not much Welsh-speaking either.

In those days Warren with St. Twynnell was good farming country. At nearby Castlemartin the famous breed of Welsh black cattle had originated. Nowadays Castlemartin is a tank and artillery range and the pleasant but unspectacular parish church of Warren is redundant.

For the next four years Charles Green continued to be taught by his father along with his brother Kenneth. He learned his first lessons in responsibility and leadership from his senior position in a large growing family. When his parents went on holiday alone to north Carmarthenshire in 1876, they left Charles to keep an eye on the smaller children in the charge of the servants at the vicarage. Charles was expected to forward to his parents the letters that they wanted to receive while they were on holiday. He was praised by his mother for his reply to her letter although, as one would expect from a twelve-year old boy, it was "very short". Charles was curtly reminded that he had forgotten "to put in the Castlemartin letter" and he was told to pass on love and kisses to "Sebert, Elsie, Eric, Wilfrith and the sweet baby". The sweet baby, Edith, had been born at Warren in September 1875 and Charles was to remain close to her throughout his life. At the time of his mother's letter in 1876, Sebert was eight years old; Elsie was seven; Eric was five and Wilfrith not yet four. In May 1878, when he was nearly fourteen years old, Charles left Warren to begin his more formal secondary education at the Charterhouse in Surrey.

2. In via

The Charterhouse Register records that Charles Green entered the school in Cricket Quarter 1878 and left in Cricket Quarter 1883. For those who think that there has been a tendency since the sixteenth century for pupils to spend progressively longer periods over their secondary education, it is perhaps worth noting that John Wesley, one of the most famous Carthusians, spent six years there before his election to a scholarship at Christ Church, Oxford. Wesley's Charterhouse had stood since 1611 just west of Aldersgate where the most famous English Carthusian monastery had been established in 1371. Green went to Charterhouse during a period of great expansion in the history of the school. Only six years before his admission the school had been moved to its present site near Godalming in Surrey. As one of the seven great public schools its governing body had been revised by the Public Schools Act of 1868 and greater attention was beginning to be paid to the teaching of modern languages, history and science which had previously suffered because of the privileged place of Classics in the Public School curriculum. It was nevertheless as a Classical Scholar that Green emerged from the Charterhouse in 1883.

Surrey was the county from which Green's great-grandfather Francis Green had originated, but Alfred Green probably had no other motive in sending Charles to Charterhouse than the high reputation of the school and the desire to do his best by his eldest son. The school fees were high and the Vicar of Warren could not have afforded to send his son there without the benefit of a private income. Warren was worth £254 a year, which was not beggarly for the time, but the cost of keeping Charles at Charterhouse was more than half that amount in the early years when there were six other children at home. By his third year at the school Charles had gained a senior scholarship and it was with some sense of relief that Alfred Green recorded that "out of fifteen terms eight were lightened by Charles's senior scholarship" which reduced the termly fees to a quarter of their full cost. Even so, Charles had to be withdrawn from Charterhouse in April 1883 although he had not then secured his scholarship at Keble and his house-master greatly regretted his departure.

Charles Green was one of 137 entrants to Charterhouse in 1878, twenty of whom were the sons of clergymen. One of these, Oswald Latter, later went on with Green to Keble where he became a tutor and subsequently a House Master at Charterhouse. He remained in touch with Green throughout his life. Three others from Green's group of entrants in May 1878 were to become clergymen. The Headmaster,

Haig Brown, was himself in holy orders. He came to hold Charles Green in high regard and told Green's father that "Charles' career at Charterhouse is among my most pleasant memories".

Charles was first placed in the house of Mr. Buisson but when he was a senior scholar he became a Daviesite. His housemaster, Gerald S. Davies, a Cambridge graduate, was also a clergyman and had been at Charterhouse since 1874. Davies had a high opinion of Charles Green whose school career he regarded "with nothing but pleasure and his leaving with nothing but regret".

Green's skill and delight in public debating that was to blossom when he went to Oxford, was fostered at Charterhouse in the sixth form debating society. On 14th October, 1882, Green spoke against the motion that capital punishment ought to be abolished. He contended that all burglars and murderers were essentially brutes, and consequently the sooner they were got out of the way the better. Whether through the cogency of Green's reasoning or from the unpopularity of the motion, it was heavily defeated. A fortnight later he opposed the motion that "Ghosts exist only in the imagination" and it was reported by the Carthusian that he "narrated two thrilling stories which greatly affected the audience". The following February Green appeared as the seconder of two motions: the first "that the writings of female novelists are prejudicial to the minds of the people"; the second that "this house would be glad to see public horse racing done away with", when his performance was again praised by the Carthusian. If Green shared the prejudices of most middle-class Victorians in his support of capital punishment and ghosts as well as his antipathy to talented ladies, he was no great lover of the sport of kings.

Charles Green was happy at Charterhouse and he in turn was liked and respected. It says much for his father, for Charles Green himself and for Charterhouse that after only five years there he became a scholar of Keble College, Oxford, where he was to be even happier and where he was to experience the deep influences that affected the whole future course of his life.

Oxford

When Charles Green went up to Oxford at Michaelmas 1883, Keble was a new college that had been founded only thirteen years earlier as a memorial to the great Tractarian leader who had died in 1866 and as a tribute to the Oxford Movement whose genesis was attributed to his Assize Sermon in St. Mary's Church in 1833. Keble's sermon had questioned the whole basis of the relationship between Church and State in England at the time and had asserted the Catholicity of the Church of England. Keble College, boldly designed by Butterfield in red-brick with its magnificent chapel had been established in response to the desire for a college that would assert the ideals of the Oxford

Movement. Anglicans should be able to be educated by Anglicans in an atmosphere that was free from the liberalism and secularism that had penetrated some of the other colleges. Anglican scholars of limited financial means like the young Charles Green should be able to "live economically, with a college wherein sober living and high culture of the mind could be combined with Christian training based upon the principles of the Church of England".

For a young man of Charles Green's temperament and inclinations Oxford itself and Keble college in particular was an exciting place to be. The great leaders of the Oxford Movement, Keble and Pusey were dead, but their ideas survived and their disciples were in prominent positions. The Tractarians flourished at Oxford during the years 1883-88. They continued to promote the ideal of *ecclesia anglicana* as a branch of the Catholic Church. They were no longer afraid of the English Reformation which they enhanced by a deeper understanding of the Catholicity of the Book of Common Prayer. The Tractarians made ecclesiastical history a respectable academic discipline and in William Bright the Regius Professor of ecclesiastical history they possessed one of their most able exponents.

If the Tractarians at this time were concerned to deepen the spirituality and increase the awareness of catholicity within the Church of England, they were no less concerned to interpret the findings of Biblical scholarship and higher criticism to their contemporaries although older Tractarians like H.P. Liddon, Pusey's biographer, had disapproved of such things. If *Essays and Reviews* was the controversial volume that had heralded Green's birth, it was the volume of essays that appeared as *Lux Mundi* in 1889 that represented the best teaching of the Tractarians of his university days.

The leading lux of *Lux Mundi* was Charles Gore, who became the first principal of Pusey House soon after Green went to Keble, but other contributors were Gore's close friend the Warden of Keble, E.S. Talbot and the sub-warden, Walter Lock who wrote a biography of Keble and was one of Green's tutors. The history tutor at Keble was the Church historian, Henry Offley Wakeman. We have at the hands of Hensley Henson, an opponent of Anglo-Catholicism, a most sincere tribute to this company of Tractarians who graced Oxford at this time: "I became acquainted with Henry Wakeman, a devout and scholarly Tractarian, through whom I came to know the leaders of Oxford Churchmanship, the Warden of Keble, Dr. Talbot; Canon Bright, and Charles Gore, then Head of the Pusey House. I was never wholly accordant with the type of Churchmanship which they represented, but it attracted and impressed me. For the first time Anglicanism appealed to me as a reasonable, coherent and attractive version of Christianity".[3]

Among Green's personal friends at Oxford were the historian Charles Oman, a fellow of All Souls whom he met through the Oxford

Union Society, and A.R. Whitham who later became vice-principal of Cuddesdon Theological College where Green stayed on several occasions although he himself never went to a theological college.

It could be claimed with some justification that anyone who was at Keble College in those years had no further need of a theological college. Of the fifty-six young men who entered the college in Green's year, thirty-five became clergymen and at least two of them were future bishops. Among the students who were already resident at Keble, the one whose friendship was to mean most to Green in later life was Beresford James Kidd, a future warden of the college. Like his great mentor William Bright, Kidd was a historian of the early Church. He took a keen interest in Green's future career and when he wrote to congratulate Green upon becoming the first Bishop of Monmouth in 1921, Kidd recalled Green's resolve "to devote yourself when you went down, to the Church in Wales ... and I can see you now, standing in front of a folio Bible in Welsh placed on a large reading desk, in your room at the end of the Chapel Buildings and declaiming it aloud so as to get a mastery over that tongue..."

This picture of Green as a very earnest young man is borne out by his activities in the Oxford Union of his day. His friend Charles Oman had become Librarian of the Union Society after taking his first in history in 1883, but Green was Librarian and President of the Union while he was still preparing for finals in Greats. Green became a skilful debater in print and in speech and he had a very clear mind that expressed itself skilfully and effectively. Green's experience at the Union debates helped him to think on his feet and gave him much greater confidence and his Union activity seems to have been his major source of relaxation at Oxford.

With Charles Oman and Griffith Boscawen, Green edited the Oxford Review from the beginning of 1885 until he left Oxford. The review faithfully recorded the debates in which Green spoke at the Union and also in the Keble Debating Society where he failed by one vote in February 1885 to secure acceptance of the motion that "some modifications ought to be effected in the relations between Church and State". Lest this apparently uncharacteristic gesture should be misconstrued, it should be added that he condemned "the schemes of the Liberationists" and deplored "the indecisive attitude taken up by one of the leading members of the Opposition on the question of Disestablishment". Thus Green argued at the Union debate in October 1885 when he received unanimous support for his views. His censure referred to Gladstone's ambivalent attitude towards the disestablishment of the Church in Wales at that time. Unlike Gladstone, Green never wavered over his opposition to Welsh disestablishment. In later life he admitted that disestablishment had not in fact brought the disaster that Welsh churchpeople once feared, but we shall return to that later.

The Tories were preeminent in the Union Society at Oxford while Green was there and it was during that time that his commitment to the Conservative Party was established. In May 1885 at the end of Gladstone's second ministry, Green spoke in favour of a motion regretting that the Government had so long delayed the declaration of war with Russia. The ayes easily had it at the end of the debate although Gladstone believed as strongly as the Conservatives in the independence of Afghanistan which had been at risk through Russian aggression. The Tory hand at the Union was strengthened when Lord Robert Cecil was elected President in June 1885, the month in which his father Lord Salisbury became Prime Minister.

In the Keble Debating Society on 30th November, 1885, Green moved that "Reaction is not the essence of Toryism", a motion that was easily carried by 23 votes to 5. As a leading figure in the Oxford University Habitation of the Primrose League, Green was busily engaged in preparation for its annual dinner at Oxford in March 1886. In the same month he moved in a Union debate that "this house regards with complete distrust the foreign policy of the Radical School". In May 1886, during Gladstone's brief third ministry, Green spoke in favour of the Union protest against Gladstone's proposals to establish Home Rule in Ireland "as tending to the disintegration of the British Empire".

A month later Gladstone's first Home Rule bill for Ireland failed in the Commons. Two months later a tithe war began in Wales because the Nonconformists thought it iniquitous to have to support a Church to which they did not belong and the Agricultural depression in north Wales added to the financial burden that was imposed by the payment of tithe. In November 1886 the Oxford Union debated the motion that "this house strongly disapproves of the anti-Tithe Agitation". Green, whose father was then a rector in north Wales, spoke in the debate and showed how clearly he understood the relationship between the vexed question of the payment of tithe and the mounting pressures for the disestablishment of the Church in Wales. Green said that he would go so far with the opponents of the motion "as to say that the clergy should reduce the tithe in the same proportion as the owners did the rents". He did not say that some Welsh clergymen had already voluntarily agreed to rebates because of the hardship that was caused to many tenant-farmers by the payment of tithe at a time of agricultural depression. Green asserted that the Church's right to exact tithes resolved itself into the question, "Were the original donors justified in laying a tax upon land?" a question to which he was often to return in his later speeches in the cause of Church Defence at Aberdare.

The growing strength of Nonconformity in Wales during the second half of the nineteenth century and the political support that the Nonconformists gave to the Liberals produced a reaction that drove many Anglicans in Wales into the arms of the Conservative Party. Not all Anglicans were Tories and some regretted that "the cause of the Church was linked with Toryism",[4] but Green was not one of them. What is more, he had an antipathy to the Nonconformist conscience as it sought the realisation of its aims through the Liberal Party. In the case of alcoholic beverages, Green preferred the brewers to the total abstainers and he strongly opposed the motion before the Union in December 1887 which earnestly desired total abstinence among all classes "in view of the widespread evils of drink". Green's opposition to the Nonconformists was intensified by his political differences with them. He knew the power of the pulpit, particularly in rural Wales, to influence people's political attitudes.

In an article in the Oxford University Review in October 1885 Green had claimed that "representations of the local preachers" in Wales had produced the "very one-sided result of the election of 1880" when the Liberals had been returned to power and twenty-nine of the thirty-three Welsh constituencies had returned a Liberal member. Green claimed that most of the congregations in Wales were drawn from the lower middle-class of society "which knows just enough to desire independence of any external administration, or of the rule of the educated imposed from without, but has not that discernment which could pierce the false conclusions drawn by their political guides". He believed that the intellectual ability of the Nonconformist clergymen outside the towns was little better than their congregations and that they were therefore "unable to rise above the garbled arguments furnished by party papers or sectarian shortsightedness". These were indeed strong words pronounced with all the dogmatic confidence of a twenty-one year old son of the Established Church. One certainly detects in the young Charles Green no youthful spirit of rebellion, but rather a desire to embrace all the prejudices and certainties of the class and profession in which he had been nurtured. Green longed to be ordained as a priest to serve in the Church in Wales, but whenever he spoke of Wales at Oxford he only echoed the social and political bitterness that existed between the Church and Chapel of his day. Green shared the religious outlook of Gladstone and Gore but not their politics. Had he done so, he would have been better able to understand Welsh Nonconformity, but he would have been a less effective protagonist of Church Defence.

Green was devoted to the Church in Wales while still an undergraduate. His paternal ancestors were English but his father spent the whole of his ministry in the Church in Wales. Wales was the land of Green's mother if not of his fathers. The enthusiasm that he had for the Welsh Church was infectious. His friend, Gilbert Cunningham Joyce, son of a Vicar of Harrow and a sharper mind than Green's, eventually succeeded Green as Bishop of Monmouth.

After the usual four years of study, Green took a second in Greats (Classics) in the summer of 1887. He remained at Keble for a further year while he read widely in Theology and prepared for ordination. Another twenty years were to elapse before Green became a bachelor and subsequently a doctor of divinity. By 1888 his father had moved from Pembrokeshire to Montgomeryshire in the diocese of St. Asaph. Green's brother Kenneth was ordained by the Bishop of St. Asaph, Alfred George Edwards in 1889 at the first ordination by the new bishop at the beginning of his forty-five year tenure of that diocese. Oxford associations decreed that Charles Green should go elsewhere, though he later confessed that his first curacy was not the first for which he had applied. Partly through the influence of the Cowley Fathers, or Society of St. John the Evangelist, to whom Green used to make his confession, he was put into touch with the Vicar of Aberdare, Richard Bowen Jenkins. Richard Meux Benson, the founder of the S.S.J.E., had conducted a retreat in the parish of Aberdare in 1886 and had initiated a daily celebration of the Eucharist in the parish. Less than two years later, Charles Green arrived to serve his title. He was made deacon at the Trinity ordination, 1888, by Richard Lewis, Lord Bishop of Llandaff, and his first sphere of work as an assistant curate was the district of Cwmbach in the Parish of Aberdare. His work centred on the church of St. Mary Magdalene.

Large industrial parishes like Aberdare were greatly favoured by the Anglo-Catholic clergy at the time. In the year that Green went to his assistant curacy at Aberdare, the Warden of Keble, E.S. Talbot, became Vicar of Leeds. By 1888 Anglo-Catholic priests were making names for themselves in similar parishes throughout the country. Many of them were priests of the people with a common touch and a social outlook that Charles Green never possessed but Aberdare, though industrial, was very different from Leeds or Landport or east London, and Green was no slum priest. He retained a great love of Oxford and especially of Keble College. He remained a life-long member of the Keble Association and he took great pride in his election to an honorary fellowship of Keble after he had become Archbishop of Wales. In the meantime Green applied at Aberdare the lessons that he had learned at Oxford and he continued to learn from a great Church parish in the making and in the shaping of which his own contribution was to be by no means insignificant.

3. Aberdare

a. *Assistant curate at Cwmbach*

After his ordination on 10th June, 1888 Charles Green moved into lodgings at Cwmbach. The church of St. Mary Magdalene for which he was responsible, had been consecrated as recently as 1882 although the coal-mining community at Cwmbach was much older than that. Cwmbach could indeed claim to be in the vanguard of social and economic reform since the first co-operative store in Wales had been opened there in 1860.

At Cwmbach Green quickly settled down to the life of an unmarried assistant curate, and we may easily picture him there assiduously preparing his sermons and addresses in his Victorian room. After one year's apprenticeship as a deacon, he was ordained to the priesthood at Trinity 1889. That was the year in which he first began to keep a detailed account of everything that he did. Green kept up his diary most conscientiously for every day of every year of his life from 1889 until 1944. The last entry in his diary is for Monday 10th April, 1944 which was, appropriately Easter Monday. He had just resigned as Archbishop of Wales and he died a month later.

Green's diaries now fill two cardboard boxes at the National Library of Wales, Aberystwyth. They are written from start to finish in that precise and neat handwriting that matured with age and reflects the discipline and clarity of the mind that it expresses. Green wrote his diaries as if he would have them at hand on the Day of Judgement as evidence of how he had spent every moment of his waking life, but they make very dull reading since the entries simply record lists of engagements and itineraries. That does not mean that they were used as engagement books to remind him in advance of what he had to do, because they were obviously written up after the events had taken place. It does mean that Green never allowed himself the luxury of recording in his diary any opinion upon any event or person with whom he came into contact. Only once during his fifty-five years as a diarist did he record for posterity his judgement upon any matter, and that was when he visited the parish of Trefeglwys as Bishop of Bangor on Sunday 13th January, 1929 at 3 p.m. when he "inspected" the mission church at Llawryglyn and recorded (in parentheses) that the church was "in a shocking condition".

We are rushing ahead. When Green began his first extant diary, he was the most junior of six assistant curates of the parish of Aberdare. He was paid in quarterly instalments an annual salary of less than £120 which was fairly generous by the standards of the time. A cartoon in *Punch* in March 1909 portrayed a curate struggling to exist on £120 a year as living in abject poverty, but the cartoonist's curate had a wife and six children, whereas the unmarried Charles Green would probably have been one of the richest men in Cwmbach at a time when the best-paid collier would have been lucky to earn a pound a week.

When Green went to Aberdare he was a stranger to industrial South Wales having known only the rural areas, but he wasted no time in getting to know the people of Cwmbach. He was a diligent visitor in their homes and he was not slow to see for himself under what conditions the men worked. On Thursday 1st August, 1889 the young diarist recorded that he had been down Llettyshenkin Pit in the afternoon, on a day that had started with Matins in church at 7.30 a.m. followed by a celebration of the Eucharist after which he had prepared a sermon that he preached that evening at Evensong in Cwmbach at 7.30 p.m. He then went on to a Church Club committee meeting at 9 p.m. If the work of the coal-miners was more arduous and dangerous and less remunerative, the hours of the assistant curate were even longer than theirs.

As well as the women at home and the men in work, Green's pastoral care extended also to the children at school and Cwmbach had a National School where Charles Green quickly became a familiar figure and where he frequently taught a lesson at the beginning of the school day.

In his first years at Aberdare, Green seems to have taken only short holidays and often from Monday to Saturday only, to avoid being away on Sundays. In September 1889, he stayed with his uncle Francis Green, at St. David's, but in 1891 he set off to his beloved Oxford accompanied by H.R. Johnson, the senior curate of Aberdare and future warden of St. Michael's College. They stayed with Green's friend Charles Oman at All Souls and they later went on to Cuddesdon to stay with another friend, A.R. Whitham, at the theological college.

In 1893 when Green had been at Cwmbach for five years, the Vicar of Aberdare resigned through ill-health to take a smaller living in the diocese of St. David's. Sir William Thomas Lewis, later Lord Merthyr, a prominent churchman at Aberdare and agent for the Marquis of Bute who held the advowson, recommended that Charles Green should succeed Richard Bowen Jenkins as Vicar of Aberdare. Green was duly nominated to the Bishop who was very happy about the appointment since it was what the previous incumbent had wanted, and Green was instituted by the bishop and inducted in the small parish church of St. John the Baptist by the rural dean on 29th May, 1893. Charles Green's area of responsibility had now widened considerably although he was not yet twenty-nine years old.

b. Vicar of Aberdare

In mentioning the nineteenth century parish of Aberdare one needs to be very precise about dates since the parish had an amoeba-like existence reproducing itself by binary fission to keep pace with the rapidly growing population. The parish of 1850 and that of which Green became vicar in 1893 were scarcely the same. At the time of the Religious Census of 1851, the Parish of Aberdare extended from Hirwaun to Mountain Ash and centred on the small parish church of, St. John the Baptist, formerly a chapel-of-ease to the vast parish of Llantrisant. This was in fact the only proper church building in the parish in 1851, but St. Elvan's and St. Fagan's churches were already planned and worship was being conducted in three licensed rooms at Hirwaun, Aberaman and Cwmbach. By 1857 the licensed worship-rooms had developed into churches and St. Elvan's and St. Fagan's had been built. The town then had six churches and thirty-four chapels to accommodate a population that had grown rapidly in the thirty years after 1831 from just under 4,000 to more than 32,000, a higher percentage increase during those years than either Cardiff or the Aberdare Valley.

St. Elvan's church, built in 1852, had a seating capacity of just over 900 that was soon to prove inadequate. The parish church was restored in 1859 but could provide only two hundred seatings. Some of the services in the parish church were conducted in Welsh, but the church of St. Mary the Virgin (Sant Mair) was consecrated in November 1864 for the benefit of those who wanted to worship in Welsh. St. Fagan's had become a separate ecclesiastical parish in 1856 and by 1895 it had three daughter churches of its own. The separate parishes of St. Lleurwg's Hirwaun and St. Margaret's Aberaman were created in 1886 and 1889 respectively. Two more daughter churches, St. Matthew's, Abernant, an iron structure built in 1889, and St. John the Evangelist, Robertstown, opened in 1890, were added to the church of St. Mary Magdalene, Cwmbach to make a total of six churches in the re-organised parish of Aberdare of which Charles Green became vicar in 1893.

By 1893 the total population of Aberdare was over 40,000 and it was still growing. The rapid growth in population had been caused by the development of the steam-coal seams after the establishment of Britain's export trade in steam-coal with France. The Parish of Aberdare had a population that was only half that of the town and the new parish boundaries were closely defined. Most of the ecclesiastical reorganisation of Aberdare had taken place during the incumbency of Green's predecessor, Richard Bowen Jenkins, 1883-93, in whose memory the Aberdare Memorial Hall was opened in Seymour Street in 1895 on land given by Bowen Jenkins himself. Most surprisingly, Bowen Jenkins was present at the opening ceremony and declared opened the hall in his memory. In his speech he paid tribute to the work of his own predecessor, J.W. Wynne Jones, Vicar of Aberdare from 1876 until 1883, when he moved to Caernarfon. Wynne Jones himself had succeeded an illustrious predecessor, Canon J.D. Jenkins, D.D. Vicar 1870-76, who had closely identified himself with civic life in Aberdare and in whose memory the Amalgamated Society of Railway Servants, of which he was president, had placed an east window in St. Elvan's church.

Some of the problems of this age of expansion in the parish of Aberdare are highlighted in the manuscript diaries of David Griffith who was an assistant curate there for six years after 1877. Griffith had been a student at St. David's College, Lampeter, but he was not a graduate and he never became an incumbent. Much of what he wrote was jaundiced and commonplace, but his diaries are invaluable for their insights into the tensions that existed in Aberdare between Welsh and English; between those who did not like ceremonial and those who introduced Anglo-catholic theology and its accompanying impedimenta, and between the Christianity of the rich man in his castle and the poor man at his gate. Griffith's diaries also reveal the difficulty of getting assistant curates to work in the large industrial parishes at that time and the loneliness and the poverty that were the lot of some curates in such parishes.

By 1880, Griffith was tired of serving as assistant curate throughout the parish and he wanted an area for which he could be personally responsible. On 23rd September, 1880 he claimed that the "want of the Welsh flock is a pastor of their own as under former vicars" but when he was given charge of the Welsh church, Griffith soon grew weary of the responsibility. He writes of the puritanism of the Welsh congregation and the influence of the "chapelisers" who wanted to turn Sant Mair into a cave of Adullam from all the Welsh chapels in Aberdare.

Griffith was a strange tormented soul. He bewailed his loneliness but when a full staff of assistant curates arrived, he soon found himself in disagreement with them. In 1880 Griffith himself was conducting Welsh prayer meetings at St. Mair's, which he describes as "very warm gatherings-happy-with two or three men engaging in prayer— often followed by Baptism services — congregation joining in heartily in singing Welsh hymns and repeating last two lines ever so many times". This contrasted wildly with the policy of the Vicar, Wynne Jones, and the other curates. On Saturday 21st May, 1881, Griffith confided in his diary that he had suffered a week of "unusual mental depression" because the Vicar had introduced "readers in surplices" into St. Mary's church on the previous Sunday evening in Griffith's absence. "Curates should be consulted as well as commanded", he exclaims, and the Vicar's action so upset him that he did no visiting all the week, but "worshipped God twice a day in his sanctuary, throughout the week. The holy calm soothed our weary soul".

On 22nd September, 1881, Griffith was complaining, "English organists are the death of our Welsh Psalmody", and on the following day he made a review of life in the parish during the previous year in which he claimed that St. Elvan's was in its "advanced phase of Ritualism". On the feast of St. John the Baptist, 1881, a "high celebration" of the Holy Communion had been held for the first time in the parish church for its patronal festival with celebrant, deacon and sub-deacon. Griffith complained that the "ritual was entirely out of harmony with the surroundings — might suit gay St. Elvan's but suited not plain and primitive St. John's. The Vicar gave a graphic account of the Church in the Wilderness ... which as a fiction was fine, but as a fact was failure".

It might be said that 1881, seven years before Charles Green became an assistant curate there, was the year when Tractarianism entered its advanced stage in Aberdare. The three new deacons, H.R. Johnson, A.E. Hyslop and J.H. Lloyd were joined by A.E. Campbell, a future bishop of Glasgow and Galloway, in the summer. Another curate in the parish, H.E. Thursby excited Griffith's ire by preaching a sermon on "Holy Mary, mother dear", and Campbell drove Griffith to apoplexy with a sermon on "the power of Priesthood" and drew from him a long lament about the Romanizing tendencies at St. Elvan's.

The advanced churchmanship of the new curates was less out of place in the parish of Aberdare during these years than the sad loftiness of the touchy David Griffith. Aberdare had experienced the Oxford Movement almost first-hand when Evan Lewis had been its Vicar for seven years after 1859. Lewis's elder brother had been received into the Roman Catholic Church with Newman in 1845. Evan Lewis had been the founder of St. Mair's church and he had also translated a number of hymns into Welsh.

David Griffith left Aberdare in 1883 and Evan Lewis became Dean of Bangor in 1884. The choir of St. Mair's wore surplices for the first time at Evensong in Advent 1885 and vestments were worn for the first time in the parish church at Christmas 1887. In 1889 altar lights were first used at St. Elvan's, but it was not until November 1902 that Green introduced the vestments for celebrant, deacon and sub-deacon at St. Elvan's and he said that they would only be worn at the greater festivals and at the early celebrations on ordinary Sundays. By that he meant that they would be worn at the service of Holy Communion at eight o'clock on Sunday mornings when most able-bodied people would have been present to make their communions. Only on the first Sunday of each month was there a Sung Eucharist or Choral Celebration of the Holy Communion, as it was called, at St. Elvan's at 11 o'clock, and on the other Sundays of the month at that time the service was Sung Matins, which was probably the only service offered at that hour in most parish churches in Britain on every Sunday of the year before the first world war. While the parish of Aberdare was a pace-setter in liturgical changes, it would be foolish to imagine that the whole Parish-Communion movement of later decades was anticipated in Aberdare during Green's incumbency. The practice of weekly Sung Eucharists in parishes at more convenient times for parishioners than eight o'clock on a Sunday morning was unknown while Green was Vicar of Aberdare and he would have regarded the convenience aspect as sheer laziness.

Green used the advantages of six churches and as many assistant curates in the parish to establish a Choral Communion at eleven o'clock in Welsh or English in three churches on three different Sundays of the month. In fairness to Green and *pace* David Griffith, he had services of the Holy Communion in the parish church on two Sundays of the month and at Abernant on the other two Sundays, when there were no lights on the altar and only a simple surplice was worn by the celebrant. He thus sought to be fair to all shades of churchmanship. The liturgical use of incense and the carrying of lights in procession in public worship, proscribed by the two Archbishops in 1899, were never introduced by Green.

The Tractarian movement in Aberdare, as elsewhere, meant much more than mere ceremonial and one of the main tasks of Green and his immediate predecessors was Christian education and the development of the spiritual lives of the parishioners. Building on his predecessors' foundations, Green helped to develop one of the best 'Church' parishes in the old diocese of Llandaff, but how much was Aberdare a 'Church' town during Green's incumbency? The question is relevant to the contribution that Green was able to make to the place of the Church in the community.

The most colourful personality in the town of Aberdare at the time of Green's birth had been Dr. Thomas Price, the controversial Baptist minister first of Carmel and then of Calfaria, an enormous Welsh chapel which boasted over a thousand members. Price involved himself fully in civic affairs and he died at Aberdare after a ministry of forty-two years there within months of Green's arrival in the town. Only twice during Green's long incumbency at Aberdare did the total number of Easter communicants of the parish exceed a thousand, and that is a measure of the relative strength of his six churches compared with Calfaria under Dr. Price. If Price was John the Baptist to the town of Aberdare, then Green was not the messiah.

Even in such a successful 'Church' parish as Aberdare the real numerical strength lay with the nonconformists. Like all the others on the south Wales coal-field, Aberdare was a nonconformist town. The figures for the triennial election of the Aberdare School Board in 1901, when there were fifteen candidates for thirteen seats, reveal that the most popular clergyman in Aberdare at the time was still the Baptist minister of Calfaria, James Griffiths, while Green, Canon Johnson of

St. Michael's College, and the Vicar of Aberaman competed for bottom places of those who were elected.

Green always believed that Church leaders should not interfere and certainly should not intervene in social or political disputes. The extent to which he preserved a genuinely neutral position in such matters is certainly questionable, but in 1893 he was sufficiently surprised by the arrival of the army in Aberdare to record "Aberdare on strike" in red ink at the top of the appropriate page in his diary. The Hauliers' strike had spread to Aberdare in support of the Rhondda Hauliers, and on Tuesday 22nd August the officers of the Bedfordshire Regiment visited Green and he later preached to them in the parish church from a suitable passage describing the military exploits of Joshua.

Troops and police were dispersed over the coal-field to protect those miners who were willing to work in spite of the strike. The strikers demanded a twenty per cent increase in the terms of the agreement of the sliding scale which had related wages to the selling price of coal since 1876. Five employers and five miners' representatives sat as a joint-committee to arrange the rate of wages according to the sliding scale of the price of coal. It was at best a palliative measure because it was manipulated in the interests of the employers and the vice-chairman, William Abraham (Mabon) who should have represented the miners' interests was increasingly mistrusted by them for his readiness to compromise with the wishes of the owners. Sir William Thomas Lewis, later Lord Merthyr, was one of the toughest of these and Lewis was the chairman of the sliding scale committee. The sliding scale agreement finally collapsed with the failure of the miners' six-months' strike in 1898, but the agreement limped on until 1902. 1898 was the year that marked the point of no return in industrial relations in south Wales with the end of the Lib.-Lab. compromise epitomised by Mabon, and the establishment of the South Wales Miners' Federation to replace the ineffectual local associations of workers.

The cracks had appeared in 1893. Green rightly expressed surprise that Aberdare should be on strike because industrial relations in the town were generally peaceful and usually better than the Rhonddas or even the Aberdare valley. Miners' leaders were opposed to strikes and Mabonism worked for compromise and adherence to the sliding scale. When the Hauliers' strike spread to Aberdare at the beginning of August, 1893, the local miners' agent urged the men not to join the Rhondda hauliers because they came out without notice and therefore acted illegally. They had also violated the agreement of the sliding scale.

Most history books have underestimated the significance of the strike of 1893 because it has been eclipsed by the more serious breakdown of 1898. The coal-owners stood firm and the strike had collapsed by the beginning of September although a mass meeting of strikers at Aberaman on 30th August, which began with prayer in

Welsh, claimed that the strike had not collapsed. The chairman of that meeting approved of the conduct of the police but not that of the "aristocracy of Aberdare" and he declared that "the sooner they got rid of the Bishop of Aberdare, the Bishop of Rhondda and the Archbishop of Mardy the better for them".[5] In the meantime the Aberdare magistrates had resolved to retain the troops because of disturbances and the fact that a large number of men were working where a large number were still on strike. A week later all the local collieries had returned to work and the Devon and Bedford Regiments as well as the 14th Hussars left south Wales in special trains.

The Archbishop of the Mardy, Sir William Thomas Lewis, remained unrepentant. When he was asked his opinion of the strike he said that it had been unique because the colliers of Aberdare came out on strike for the first time without giving notice. As President of the emergency committee of the Monmouthshire and South Wales Coalowners Association, he had refused to deviate from the terms of the sliding scale agreement and he refused to assent to the proposition that miners' wages were very low at that time. He claimed that men could earn between thirty and forty shillings a week.

The future Archbishop of Wales was soon to have an industrial archbishop as a father-in-law. In the year when his clerical son-in-law had been born, Lewis had become mineral agent to the Bute Estate and the Mardy was part of that estate. Lewis married the daughter of a colliery-owner and he himself acquired control of the pits in the lower Rhondda later known as 'Lewis Merthyr' as well as managing the Bute pits. Lewis sank a pit at Senghenydd where the terrible mining disaster occurred in 1913. In 1880 Lewis had become acting trustee to the Bute estate and had expanded its docks in Cardiff. Knighted in 1885, made a baronet in 1896 and raised to the peerage in 1911, Baron Merthyr of Senghenydd was one of the most powerful coal magnates in south Wales. He had two sons and six daughters.

Katharine Mary was his eldest child. She was exactly the same age as Charles Green and he proposed marriage to her in a letter which he wrote at four o'clock in the morning of Tuesday 2nd August, 1898, after he had visited his parents at Halkyn in Flintshire for a fortnight to think about it. At seven o'clock that morning he celebrated the Eucharist and he said Matins half an hour later. His proposal was accepted by Katharine, whom he called Kitty, at 10.30 a.m. on the same day, but the engagement was not publicly announced until 10th August. Most of the south Wales coalfield had been on strike since March. It was a world of poverty, starvation and soup-kitchens. The coal-owners stood firm. The men returned to work at the beginning of October without having achieved one of their objectives. At the Mardy preparations went ahead for the marriage that was planned for the following January.

Charles Green married Kitty at St. Elvan's church on 18th January, 1899. Two days earlier he had received a wedding gift from his parishioners of £200. On the morning of the wedding he celebrated the Eucharist as usual at 7 a.m. and this was followed by Matins. The entry in his diary for that day is characteristic of the man. He recorded that he "packed during the morning at the Vicarage. Married Kit at 2.30 p.m. Left Aberdare at 4.40 p.m. Reached Bristol at 8 p.m. Spent night at Clifton Down Hotel. Said Evensong in rooms about 10 p.m." On the following day Green "said Matins in rooms at 10 a.m. Left Clifton Down Station at 11.04. Arrived at Salisbury 1.5. Inspected Cathedral 1.30-3.15. Lunched at White Hart Hotel 3.30. Left Salisbury 5.30 p.m. arrived at Southampton 7 p.m. Stayed at L. and S.W. Hotel. Said Evensong in rooms 9.15 p.m." Only Green could have "inspected" a Cathedral for nearly two hours on the day after he had married. The Victorian preciseness about time would have seemed less strange to those who lived in the Railway Age than it does to us who pretend to live in the age of the train, but Green carried that preciseness into everything that he did.

The precise order of service that Green compiled for his wedding included the instructions that the choir should "proceed from the vestry to the choir stalls at 2.30 p.m. punctually" and that "immediately the bride's carriage reaches the outer door of the north porch, the choir and congregation shall stand and (after one chord on the organ) shall sing Hymn 271: "O Jesus, I have promised". Such preciseness was a familiar feature of all the services that Green subsequently compiled for use by the Church in Wales and which reached their apogee in the Enthronement Service for the first Archbishop of Wales in 1920. Green's reign at Aberdare was characterised by the precise but unfussy directions that were recorded for posterity in the Log Book which he inherited from his predecessor and in the Directory for the use of the Vicar of Aberdare which, among other things, commands the curate in charge of the parish church to "see that the vestry clock is wound regularly and that it keeps time regularly with St. Elvan's church clock". Similarly the Communion chalices were never to be filled to the top and the "contents of the two smaller chalices together exactly equal the contents of the largest chalice; when each is filled to a point ¾ inch from the top. The contents of the largest chalice will suffice for ninety communicants. The contents of the medium-sized chalice (Mary Johnson memorial) will suffice for 55 communicants: the contents of the smallest will suffice for 35 communicants, and $55 + 35 = 90$. C.A.H. Green!

The former Vicar of Aberdare, Richard Bowen Jenkins, had officiated at the wedding and most of the honeymoon was spent on the Isle of Wight. Charles Green and his bride had returned to London by Sunday 5th February. Green went alone to All Saints' Margaret Street for Matins and Sung Eucharist on that Sunday morning since Kitty was not well enough to go with him, but she joined him for Evensong at St. Paul's in the afternoon to hear a sermon from the Bishop of Stepney. Not satisfied with that, they went on to a second Evensong at St. Alban's Holborn where the famous Anglo-catholic priest Father Stanton held sway. On the following Sunday their sermon-tasting took them to Westminster Abbey to hear Charles Gore preach.

When they returned to Aberdare, Green and his wife lived for a while at Mardy House because the Vicarage was being renovated and enlarged to suit Mrs. Green's tastes. The area of floor-space that then had to be carpeted was regretted by more than one of Green's successors at the Vicarage.

At the end of the summer of that year, Green and Kitty visited his parents at Halkyn and they also stayed in other parts of north Wales including Criccieth, the home of a more famous contemporary Lloyd George, who was to be thrust into the limelight a month later through his opposition to the Boer War. For most of their time at Aberdare Green and his wife went abroad for their holidays and usually for a month to Switzerland or Austria or north Italy and sometimes to Scotland. They were not poor, and thanks to her father, she had far more money than he, but they were generous to the Church throughout their lives and they contributed more than anyone else, except Lord Merthyr himself, to local church restoration and especially to the enlarging of St. Elvan's. In 1900, when they had been married for more than a year, they made the significant decision to give one tenth of their income, after payment of income tax, to the Church. They continued to do this although the parish of Aberdare was never a rich living even after one hundred pounds a year had been added to the stipend through a generous endowment by Sir William Thomas Lewis in May 1904.

Green also made generous financial contributions towards the cost of the education of his youngest brother, Sebald, sixteen years his junior, who was subsequently killed in command of H.M.S. Glowworm on the River Dvina in Russia during the first world war. Sebald died unmarried as did Eric, the fourth son, who was assassinated by a Muslim fanatic in India in March 1900.

After he and his wife had settled down at the vicarage, Green was able to continue the work of consolidation in Christian education and spiritual development in the parish that he had started in 1893. He devoted several years to this task until his administrative burden was increased in 1902 when he became Rural Dean of the deanery of Aberdare and he was responsible for the general oversight of the parishes from Hirwaun to Penrhiwceiber.

No one was more conscious than Green that Church teaching meant much more than mere ceremonial, or a kind of nonconformity "in drag". To develop the spiritual lives of his parishioners a daily celebration of the Holy Communion had been initiated in the parish as long ago as 1886 after R.M. Benson of Cowley had conducted a retreat there. The first parish mission had been conducted in 1890 by such famous missioners as V. Stuckey Coles and Cyril Bickersteth. The second parish mission was conducted in 1898. For a whole year before this mission Green and his colleagues visited every person in the parish to find out what the need of each might be and what help could be offered. Quiet days for lay Church workers became an annual event in the parish. Green attached great importance to these, and the quality of the preparation that he made for these quiet days may be illustrated by the following quotation from the leaflet which Green circulated to every Church worker in preparation for the Quiet Day in October 1896: "It is very commonly supposed that God only expects us to live virtuous lives — that is, to keep ourselves decent in behaviour and free from sins that would be condemned by every respectable person. Of course, to lead an industrious, honest, pure, temperate and generous life is what every man should do. Every good Heathen would say that such a life was the only life worthy of Man. But it is a great mistake to think that such a life is sufficient for a Christian. A "virtuous life" is a life which does not offend the ordinary conscience of men. People who are not Christians can do this much. But a "Christian life" is a life which springs out of a living FAITH in and love for, our Lord Jesus Christ. Our lives are only Christian lives so far as they are lived out of love for him, and in dependence upon his mercy and grace..."

The task of Christian education was carried on through the work of guilds, clubs and Bible-classes, and by week-night services at St. Elvan's, when addresses were delivered on carefully planned subjects, and there were, of course, the Church schools and the Parish Sunday Schools. The number of scholars in the Welsh and English Sunday Schools in the parish rose sharply from 813 in 1895 to 1471 in 1898. The number of Sunday School teachers also increased from 61 in 1895 to 107 in 1898. During the next ten years there was a gradual decline in scholars and teachers. Even so, in 1904 there were 1291 scholars on the books, but it was reported that only 63% attended regularly, and there were 77 teachers. In 1908 there were 1187 scholars and 73 teachers.

If the numbers of scholars and teachers are impressive by modern standards, so too was the Sunday School syllabus. The lessons for the year were carefully planned. Those for 1901-2 were intended to teach the Christian Faith set forth in the Apostles' Creed and illustrated by passages of Scripture. There was much repetition of the psalms and other passages of Scripture as well as the Catechism, and every year it was clearly ordered that the collect for the Sunday was to be part of the repetition on every Sunday in addition to what was otherwise specified. After Green became Rural Dean of Aberdare in 1902, a syllabus on similar lines was drawn up for the whole Deanery Sunday School Association.

The death of Queen Victoria on 22nd January, 1901 was a significant reminder of the end of the nineteenth century. Under the heading 'The Funeral of the late Queen Victoria, 2nd February, 1901', Green pasted into the Vicar's Log Book the account that he had cut from the *Merthyr Express*. This was not however an account of Her Majesty's official funeral service, but it described what had happened at Aberdare, and from this account an observer from overseas might have imagined that Queen Victoria had been buried at Aberdare. All business had stopped. The pits were idle and business premises were closed until four o'clock when the pubs. and clubs were opened. The streets were deserted in the morning and flags flew at half mast. In the afternoon the streets were lined with spectators while the procession of public bodies passed to St. Elvan's church while the bells tolled. St. Elvan's was packed with people for the service which was conducted by the Vicar who also preached a sermon from St. Matthew chapter 11, verse 28: "Come unto me all ye that labour and I will give you rest". At the end of the sermon the vast congregation sang the hymn, "Now the labourer's task is o'er". All irony passed unobserved. The service was fully choral and three anthems were sung as well as the psalms for the day.

The year 1901 was also a watershed in the life of Charles Green. By the following year he had become Rural Dean of Aberdare and was responsible for a wider area. It was characteristic of Green that his first address as Rural Dean to his chapter of clergy on 2nd April, 1902 was later published as "The Office of a Rural Dean, with an appendix showing the old deaneries of the Diocese of Llandaff". In this pamphlet Green traced the history of the Rural Dean's office from its origin in France between 816 and 1222 until it reached Britain through the Normans. "This thought" said Green to the Aberdare clergy in 1902, "that behind our Chapter to-day in this part of the Diocese of Llandaff there lies a history of nearly one thousand years, will doubtless lead us to a higher estimate of the value of these meetings".

At this time Green became concerned about the threat that was posed to Christian education through the pressures that were placed upon the Church schools by the illegal refusal of the Welsh County Councils to administer the Balfour Education Act of 1902. Apart from the grants that they received through the Government, which the County Councils agreed to pay, the Church schools were supposed to receive their main financial support, under the terms of Balfour's Act, from the rates that had been collected by the County Councils. In the nonconformist controlled County Councils of Wales a revolt, that had been engineered and fomented by Lloyd George, caused the County Councils to refuse to support the Church schools from the rates and therefore a real threat was posed to the future of Church schools in Wales. Green played his full part in convening meetings of Churchpeople in the Aberdare deanery to protest against what he called "the illegal and inequitable treatment of the Church schools by the local Education Committee". On 15th February, 1905 he called a meeting of his own parishioners in the Memorial Hall to consider what Churchpeople should do "in view of the forthcoming Urban District Council Elections" and to decide what else "should be done in defence of the Church and her schools".

In March 1906, together with many others throughout the country, Green organised a petition or Memorial, as he called it, from parents of children attending Council Schools and the National Schools in the parish of Aberdare. This petition contained the signatures of 634 parents and was forwarded on 27th March, 1906 to the Right Hon. Augustine Birrell, M.P., the President of the Board of Education in the new Liberal Government. The petition, like scores of others at the time, advocated the retention of Church teaching by "Christian masters and mistresses and other teachers in regard to whom we may have some real assurance that they believe what they teach". At that time the new Education Bill was still being drafted, but the petitioners of Aberdare and elsewhere were horrified to discover at the first reading of the Bill that it included the clause that there were to be no more Church schools in the future. Birrell's Education Bill was rejected by the Lords and so it became part of the fuel to Lloyd George's fire to singe the House of Lords.

The political controversy aroused over the Church schools was conducted in Wales against the background of the Religious Revival associated with the name of Evan Roberts. This reached its zenith in the winter of 1904-5 when the Anglicans of Aberdare, as elsewhere, affected by the revival that had temporarily strengthened the main Nonconformist denominations, were conducting revival services and prayer meetings in the Memorial Hall under the auspices of the Church Mission League. In May 1905 Green organised a week of Quiet Evenings with meditations on some "operations of the Holy Spirit" in the parish church. In a printed leaflet to his parishioners advertising these quiet evenings, Green reminded them that the Archbishop of Canterbury had written to the Bishops in Wales to express the hope that Churchpeople would unite in prayer at Whitsuntide that "God the Holy Spirit may indeed make the fire of loyal devotion glow in us with fresh intensity". Quiet evenings with meditations were much more in Green's style than revival services. The Religious Revival had no noticeable effect upon the Parish of Aberdare. So much of Green's work at this time was conducted in an atmosphere of defensiveness of the Church's position in her schools and in opposition to Nonconformist threats through Liberal legislation that it is small wonder that relations with the Nonconformists were at such a low ebb.

After the threat to the Church schools came the threat of disestablishment with its attendant evil of disendowment. So much has been written on the campaign for Welsh Church Disestablishment that it hardly seems necessary to add to the tomes and the pamphlets "which can be weighed by the ton"[6] produced during the campaign and still being produced. Green himself contributed to this ton of pamphlets by publishing several addresses that he made during these years. He was not in the category of main-stream Church defender, reserved for Bishops Edwards and Owen, and he was not even an archdeacon at the time, but he was a good historian with a very clear mind and an enjoyment of this kind of controversy. His printed addresses from this period provide clearly-argued and tightly-reasoned expositions of the Church's case and they show no trace of factious oratory.

The Elizabethan ideal of one Church in one nation had been under fire since the seventeenth century. After the foundation of the Liberation Society in 1844, pressures mounted in Wales for the removal of the rights and privileges of the established Church of England in Wales which had the support of only a minority in Wales and was alienated from the nonconformist majority which resented its own inferior social status and the payment of the tithe-rent charge to a Church with which it lacked sympathy. That the nonconformist adherents comprised the numerical majority was confirmed by the Religious Census of 1851, and the disestablishment of the Church in Ireland in 1869 seemed to lend strength to the views of the nonconformists who found political expression for their grievances through the Liberal Party which was securely in control in Wales after 1880. When Gladstone eventually conceded that Wales could be treated separately from England, the way was open for serious proposals for Welsh Church disestablishment to be made, and by 1886 the nonconformist demand had been translated into a major item of Liberal policy. Even so, it was not until Gladstone had stepped down from the leadership that the first Welsh Disestablishment Bill was introduced by Asquith in April 1894, and the first Bill with any serious chance of success was in fact the third Disestablishment Bill, presented by Asquith on 26th April, 1909.

The disendowment terms of this bill were more favourable than the previous attempts to remove from the Church in Wales all the vested income that it had received before 1703. The date now proposed was 1662 and it was no longer proposed to secularize the cathedrals and the burial grounds.

In October 1909, Green read a paper to the Swansea Church Congress that was later published as *The Church's title to its endowments.* In that paper Green argued cogently that the obligation to pay tithes had not been created by the state but by those who owned the land and therefore had the right to lay a permanent charge upon it. The state, argued Green, only helps everyone to get his due, but the Church's title rests upon the donation made in perpetuity by the landowner.

Next followed the paper read at the Llandaff Diocesan Conference on 20th October, 1910, *"Self Government compatible with Establishment and Endowment"*. This had been read by Green in defence of a motion that this conference is of the opinion that a larger measure of self-government should be granted to the National Church without prejudice either to its endowments or to the existing establishment. At that stage Green had no objection to the greater autonomy of the Church in Wales, but he could see no argument in favour of disestablishment or disendowment from those who alleged that such things would bring that autonomous Church closer to the people of Wales.

Green's pamphlet on Disendowment, although scholars still read it, is simply a printed address that he delivered to a rural deanery chapter, or meeting of clergymen, on 7th November, 1911 and its conclusions are based upon the harsher disendowment terms of the bill of 1909, whereas the Bill of 1912 contained terms for disendowment that were more favourable to the Church in Wales, and subsequent amendments to that Bill produced even further concessions. There was an element of injustice in the fact that ancient endowments that had been granted for the use of the Church were appropriated for secular purposes, but the final terms of disendowment were by no means as crippling as many churchpeople thought in 1911.

On the question of Disestablishment, Green was more positive and less afraid of the potential danger from the State. Long before he became a bishop, Green firmly believed that episcopacy would guarantee the Catholicity of the Church. Bishops were of the *esse* of the Church and their authority did not derive from the government but from God. As such beneficiaries of the divine *fiat* they were under no threat from disestablishment. Green's pamphlet on Disestablishment (1911) seems to echo the sentiments of Gladstone when he wished that the Archbishop of Canterbury had not spoken at Rhyl in 1890 as if it had been proposed to disestablish the Apostles' Creed. In spite of the Bills, said Green, the fundamental order of the Catholic Church could not be changed. There would still be bishops.

The last of Green's pamphlets in this period was the paper that he read at the Llandaff Diocesan Conference at Cardiff in October 1912. This was *"The relation of the Church of England to the Church of Rome in pre-Reformation times"*. In this pamphlet Green returned to the threat of disendowment which seemed to cause him more anxiety than disestablishment. The pamphlet is really an attempt to undermine the suggestion by the Church's critics that Roman Catholics had a better claim to the land and property that the Church held in Wales before 1234 on the assumption that the pre-Reformation Church was the same as the Roman Catholic Church and therefore whatever was given to the Church before 1234 was really given to the Roman Catholic Church.

In his pamphlet Green reviewed the relationship between *ecclesia anglicana*, a phrase recurrent since 1215, and the Church of Rome. He did this in three stages. In the three centuries before the Reformation the Church of England came effectively under the jurisdiction of the Bishop of Rome. In the transition period after the Norman Conquest the King had more authority over the Archbishop and bishops and the legatine power was prohibited without the royal licence. The Constitutions of Clarendon, 1164, forbade appeals to Rome without the King's consent. As for the early period, Green argued, only once between 673 and the Conquest did Papal legates enter our land. What the Reformation abolished was the late medieval system of papal jurisdiction which had grown up after the *ecclesia anglicana* had become established. The Faith and discipline of Roman Catholics, argued Green, had become so affected by the Counter-Reformation and by the Tridentine and Vatican Councils, that it was preposterous for politicians to advance Roman Catholic claims to be the Church that received the ancient titles originally. This is a piece of ingenious Tractarian history-writing such as would have delighted Canon R.W. Dixon, whose six volumes of the History of the Church of England from the abolition of the Roman jurisdiction, Green had received as a wedding present from his friend Gilbert Joyce. Green's historical argument is perfectly respectable and one marvels at the ingenuity with which it is used to defend the Church in Wales from disendowment in what must have qualified as the most erudite of the whole ton of pamphlets produced during the disestablishment campaign.

Although disestablishment had been on the cards for fifty years before it became a reality, the Church was surprisingly late in organising effective defence at the local level. Churchpeople are rightly proud of the strength of the Hyde Park Rally on 12th June, 1912 and of the subsequent meeting in the Albert Hall. Two things are still worth mentioning about the Hyde Park Rally; that it had Welsh working class support and that the Churchpeople who were there probably had more knowledge of the history of the Church than Churchpeople have had since then. The rally owed its success to the local branches for Church Defence that had been established in the parishes, but most of those branches did not get under way until 1906 when the Liberals' unassailable political strength began to be realised.

The Aberdare branch of the Llandaff Church Defence League held its first meeting on Tuesday 13th November, 1906. Every member was given a membership card and undertook to "learn about the Church of England and to do all I can to strengthen its power for doing good" and also "to try to interest my neighbours to do the same". The Aberdare branch was strong. In the session 1907-8, with 319 paid-up members, it held nine meetings and a social gathering after Christmas. At the local level in Aberdare the threat of disestablishment was linked with the government's attack upon the Church schools. On 11th January, 1910 at a meeting of Aberdare deanery Churchpeople in the Market Hall, Aberdare, a public resolution was passed protesting against disestablishment and disendowment and "the introduction of any Education Bill which would not permanently secure for all children efficient religious instruction within school hours by properly-qualified teachers in accordance with the wishes of their parents", and the meeting appealed to all voters "to withold their votes from every candidate for Parliament who declines to give a satisfactory pledge in regard to Welsh Disestablishment and Religious Education".

The organisers for Church Defence in South Wales kept the facts of the various disendowment proposals before the people through single bulletin-sheets that were easily and quickly distributed. As Rural Dean of Aberdare Green made careful preparations for what was known as the Great Demonstration in London on 12th June, 1912. He arranged for a special train to leave Aberdare early on that day: cheap return tickets were available at 7/6d. through the local committee, and a time-table for the special train was printed and circulated together with a programme for the day's events. 775 rail-tickets were sold by the local committee which paid out 19/10d. for taxis "for conveyance of banners in London". The Great Demonstration in London was followed up by a demonstration in Cardiff on Saturday 29th June, 1912 at which the Aberdare delegation was much in evidence.

Green was the efficient chairman of the organising committee for the Monster Demonstration of Churchmen and Churchwomen in the Pavilion Mountain Ash on 28th November, 1912. The Pavilion had been chosen for this diocesan event because it was the largest hall in the diocese. Speakers included the Bishops of London and Llandaff and Sir Alfred Cripps, M.P. The event was widely publicised through printed circulars and advertisements in all the local newspapers as well as the *Western Mail.* Trains were organised to run to Mountain Ash from all parts of the diocese and the event had a tight schedule of speeches by Lord Aberdare, the chairman, three other speakers, a vote of thanks and the sending of a telegram to Asquith, McKenna and Bonar Law, within the space of two hours between a hymn and a prayer at 6 p.m. and a hymn and benediction at 8 p.m. With trains to be caught, speeches had to be exactly timed: the Bishop of London was allowed to speak from 6.35 p.m. until 7.10 p.m. since he was the principal speaker. At the end of the day, Green's committee was £8-13-11d. out of pocket for the day's expenses.

Local protest meetings, organised by the Aberdare Church Defence League, continued right up until the end of 1913. As late as July 1913 Green presided over a large meeting of Churchpeople from the Aberdare Valley in a field at Abercwmboi where he said that no-one had excelled Mr. Lloyd George in misrepresenting the Church, but they would continue to defend the Church "until it had been recognised that the right of the Church to her property was a moral and equitable right".

Aberdare was certainly a Welsh town throughout Green's incumbency, but the percentage of Welsh-speaking people was smaller during the second half of his time in Aberdare. As early as January 1901, the Welsh-speaking congregation at St. Mair's was alerted to the need to spend a lot of money on their church building which had been in a dilapidated condition for some time. The congregation decided to try to collect as much money as possible themselves before appealing to the parish at large. Later in the year they learned that about £800 would have to be spent immediately. When they had collected £253, Sir William Thomas Lewis gave them a further £100 and an appeal was made to parishioners for the rest of the money. In spite of this, a debt of £400 remained outstanding in 1903.

In the meantime the restored St. Mair's had been re-opened by the Bishop who presided at a Sung Eucharist there on Sunday 7th September, 1902 when the canon residentiary of St. David's Cathedral preached the sermon. Celebrations continued on the next day, the feast of the Nativity of the Blessed Virgin Mary, and throughout the following week. Green wrote a hymn in Welsh for the occasion and this was later published in *Emynau'r Eglwys*.

The task that faced Green in enlarging St. Elvan's church was much greater. In 1909 a committee was set up to consider whether it was advisable to enlarge St. Elvan's so that it could serve the English-speaking people who had moved into the new houses within three-quarters of a mile of the church. When Green appealed to his parishioners for financial help on 15th March, 1910, he said that three hundred extra seats were needed at St. Elvan's for the 807 new houses that had been built in the parish since he became vicar. The enlargement of St. Elvan's would cost at least £5,000, but Green and his wife promised one tenth of that amount if there were no bazaars or entertainments "and the church was enlarged in a proper manner". The restoration work began on 18th September, 1910.

The final cost of the enlargement and renovation was well over £5,000. By August 1911 a further examination of St. Elvan's had revealed the need for exterior repairs, a new heating system and evidence of dry rot in the pews! A further appeal was issued but the work was completed and the grand re-opening of the extended building took place in October 1911 while there was still a debt on it of £3,000.

In 1852 St. Elvan's had been built to accommodate 686 worshippers for £6,000. The provision of fewer than three hundred extra seats in 1911 cost £6,500. The work would never have been undertaken without Green's initiative, and the debt could not have been cleared before the first world war without the financial support of his wife's family. On 21st May, 1913, Lord Merthyr offered to give £500 towards the liquidation of the debt on condition that the congregation first raised another £500 before the end of the autumn.

Green and his wife had kept their promise to contribute £500 towards the work which had been tastefully completed to provide a new aisle and a chapel and a considerably lengthened chancel; two stained-glass windows in the chapel and additional space in the vestry. The organ was restored as well as the tower and the spire, and electric lights were installed for the first time together with a new heating system.

The economic climate had not been favourable to such an expensive project. Green's appeals for money were being made against a background of strikes and industrial unrest throughout the south Wales coalfield. These were the years of the Tonypandy riots and strikes for a minimum wage among the coalminers. The prolonged miners' strike in 1912 delayed the payment of the debt, and Green accepted no Easter Offering that year, but requested that the Easter collections at St. Elvan's should be given to the Restoration and Enlargement fund. The preacher at St. Elvan's during Lent and Holy Week had been Green's friend, Timothy Rees of the Community of the Resurrection and a future Bishop of Llandaff. It was an Easter that ended with greater happiness than usual for Green as he noted in his diary that Timothy Rees had stayed at the Vicarage and the colliers had returned to work!

The Bishop of Llandaff had consecrated the new portions of St. Elvan's on 3rd October, 1911. After describing the events that followed the Consecration service, the *Merthyr Express* said that great Vicars had worked at St. Elvan's "but it can be said with truth that the present Vicar is certainly as great and as scholarly a man as his predecessors". Green was certainly scholarly, but it is an interesting measure of the changes in social attitudes since then that it seems surprising that anyone should think it a virtue in a vicar to be scholarly. Scholarship takes time and energy and discipline, and the vicar of a busy industrial parish who was also the Rural Dean, needed all these in abundance when his parish was understaffed and short of money and his churches and schools were under threat from the government and in need of material restoration. Green did not lack energy and he organised his time so well that the years between 1906 and 1911 saw him proceed to the higher degrees of Bachelor and Doctor of Divinity at Oxford with high commendation from no less a person than Henry Scott Holland, the Regius Professor of Divinity. During 1906 and 1907, Green had published his Notes on the Churches in the Diocese of Llandaff in three parts. These Notes are a compilation of all the available manuscript evidence and Green must have spent many hours collating the evidence.

Green was fortunate that his scholarly inclinations led to no impatience with the day-to-day administration of a large parish and in no way hindered his pastoral concern. The pastoral care of his parishioners was always uppermost in his mind and he was constantly revising the visiting arrangements so that the whole parish could be visited regularly even when he was one curate short.

Green's predecessor, Bowen Jenkins, had been able to take for granted the presence of six assistant curates. In the 1880's they had all been very able priests: the most junior of them had become Bishop of Glasgow and Galloway by 1904, while the most senior, H.R. Johnson, had become the first Warden of St. Michael's theological college in 1892. St. Michael's was already training graduates for the Ministry at Abernant House when Green became Vicar of Aberdare and he greatly valued the presence of the college in the parish. He gave every encouragement to its development there.

St. Michael's College helped to supply the parish's constant need for six assistant curates to serve its various districts. Several of Green's curates came straight from the college, whereas the training that the parish of Aberdare provided for young graduates was invaluable. Two separate agreements were made between the parish and the college, on 17th August, 1893 and again on 7th February, 1895, which established a working relationship between college and parish. As a general principle it was agreed that no arrangement could be made between college and parish unless it was made by the Warden and the Vicar, and the choice of college men to work in the parish was to be made only by the Warden. The students worked under the supervision of the assistant curates in their respective districts. They were allowed to preach in the parish and to visit on one or two afternoons in the week. At church meetings they were permitted to be seen in order to "gain an insight into details of management" but they were not expected to be heard.

Of the twenty-eight assistant curates who served under Green at Aberdare, ten came to the parish from St. Michael's College, and most of them in the years between 1900 and 1906 before the college moved to Llandaff. Green's assistant curates stayed for lengths of time that varied between six months and ten years. Many of them stayed for four or five years, but one had to leave after two years because his health had broken down. It was difficult to keep six curates at a time and for one year between 1907-8, Green paid a Reader £1 a week to work at Robertstown. Sometimes the money could not be raised to pay for the sixth curate, and it was often difficult to find adequate accommodation for the curates. Until 1898, three of them lived rent-free at the Vicarage, but they had to entertain their colleagues to lunch on week-days and to supper on Sundays. In preparation for Green's impending marriage, the three curates had to leave the Vicarage in November 1898. But the main difficulty was raising enough money by quarterly subscriptions to pay the curates and their total number was reduced to four in 1900, when the pastoral work of the parish was carried out only through the generous help that was given by St. Michael's College.

Green went on sending begging letters to his parishioners for the payment of the curates' stipends until he left the parish. In spite of the difficulty of raising the money, he maintained a staff of six assistant curates for most of his time at Aberdare. The curates were necessary to serve the well-defined districts of the parish and to maintain that conscientious routine of pastoral visiting which was a hall-mark of Tractarian parishes. The priests' visits reflected a social as well as a spiritual concern for the parishioners. By administering a clothing club in their districts, the curates demonstrated the Church's concern for every aspect of people's lives, including their physical welfare. Green never allowed any shortage of money in the parish to impede the Church's work or to lower his horizons. The curates' account might be overdrawn, but so too was the Church Mission account and also that of the National Schools, but neither missionary work nor the work of the Church schools went unsupported because the money was not immediately to hand.

What contribution did Green make to the progress of the Church in Aberdare during his long reign there? In spite of an increase in the population of the parish and the consequent enlargement of St. Elvan's church, the Easter communicant figures increased hardly at all and the parish was still overwhelmingly nonconformist in allegiance to the end of Green's incumbency. Yet he established a foundation of Church life in Aberdare that was to survive until after his death, and in many respects he tried to rule his successors from the grave by all the detailed arrangements of precise administration that he had carefully bequeathed to them. With hindsight we can see that he was fortunate to have reigned at Aberdare during the last opportunity for the Church in such industrial parishes before the onrush of Marxist ideas and the increasing bitterness of industrial disputes on the coal-field gave way to the disaster of the Great War and its aftermath. Given the circumstances, Green's one and only incumbency was a great success and the parish was fortunate in its Vicar.

Long before 1914 the idea that industrial relationships could be maintained by some Christian compromise had ceased. It was largely a Nonconformist solution, associated with Mabon (William Abraham) and the early Lib.-Lab. arrangements, and, like Nonconformity itself it was most effective in the nineteenth century. Without realising it, Nonconformity in south Wales was becoming a spent force. The nonconformist demand for the disestablishment of the Church in Wales was a nineteenth century shibboleth accidentally projected into the twentieth century by political circumstances.

Modern commentators upon the disestablishment campaign have wished that Church and Dissent had co-operated more and quarrelled less, but the political alignment in Wales made co-operation unlikely: nonconformity expected support from the Liberals and the Church was thrown increasingly into the hands of the Tories who were in office for most of Green's time at Aberdare. Only the Liberal landslide of 1906 made disestablishment possible.

Green's own commitment to the Conservative Party at this stage was fairly clear. On 12th August, 1895 Green was publicly criticised by D.A. Thomas, the senior M.P. for the Merthyr constituency, in a speech at the Liberal Club in Aberdare because of a circular that Green had issued to Churchpeople before the General Election in that year. According to Thomas, Green had urged his parishioners to vote for Mr. Herbert Lewis, the eldest son of Sir William Thomas Lewis and Green's future brother-in-law. Lewis had been the unsuccessful Conservative candidate and Green's assistance was therefore dismissed by Thomas, but the M.P. thought that "a clergyman's time would be better employed in ministering to the spiritual needs of his flock than in acting as political agent to a Tory candidate".[7] Thomas also reminded his hearers that Anglicans had condemned Nonconformist ministers for engaging in politics and he claimed that the kind of activity in which Green was involved was the only sure road to ecclesiastical preferment in Wales.

The differences that separated Churchpeople from Nonconformists were wider than the political divide between their respective newspapers. The Liberal *South Wales Daily News* had given prominence to the speech by D.A. Thomas against Green. In a similar way, the Liberal *Merthyr Express* gave extensive coverage to the public meeting of Nonconformists at Aberaman in May 1894 after a man had been killed in a boxing contest at Aberdare on 17th May. It was falsely claimed that the victor had learned to box in a church club at Aberdare. The Nonconformists at the meeting rightly deplored the state of the law that made it possible for a prize fight to take place under the disguise of a boxing contest. The matter did not rest there, but was taken up again at a further meeting at Calfaria Hall, Aberdare, of representatives from fifty-one Nonconformist churches in the deanery of Aberdare. The minister of Carmel, the Revd T. Jones, stirred up the Puritanism of the Welsh Nonconformists there by reminding them that "they all knew where that thing began (hear, hear)". He said that he was sorry to hear that the referee had been a Sunday School teacher and a noble obedient son to his parents. The minister of Saron, Aberaman, where the first meeting had taken place, reminded the meeting at Calfaria that the victor had "commenced in a club connected with the Established Church in Aberdare (shame) and until he commenced attending that club he was a member of Saron Sunday School and a most promising young man".

The Puritanism displayed at that meeting at Calfaria degenerated into self-righteousness as the Revd R. Thomas, Penrhiwceiber, stated that he "was proud to think that the Nonconformist pulpit was so clean and so pure (hear, hear)". He went on to condemn guilds for young people which were damaging in their influence. He concluded by exhorting his audience to "go back to the old Puritan fervour and not give way to the low tastes of the young for football, cricket or even boxing (hear, hear)". They should "rather teach their young people that life was something more than mere recreation".[8] Thus the old Puritan work-ethic was proclaimed in an industrial society that still had plenty of work for its young people.

The incident that became known as "the fatal glove fight at Aberdare" is interesting because it illustrates that the differences between the Church and the Nonconformists in Wales during the disestablishment campaign went much deeper than politics but touched the theological disagreement about whether a Christian should be a Puritan or not.

4. Archdeacon of Monmouth

Their last years at Aberdare passed very happily for Green and his wife. Green's domestic happiness was impaired only by the death of his father on 10th December, 1911 in his retirement home at Clevedon. The Revd. A.J.M. Green, with his keen intelligence and an aptitude for foreign languages, had served the Church in Wales for fifty years, and he was buried, as he had requested, in Llangathen churchyard.

In August 1913, unaware of the changes that would shortly affect their personal fortunes and ignorant of the fact that foreign travel would never be the same again, Green and his wife travelled through Germany and Austria to Innsbruck for a month's holiday. This was the last opportunity that British subjects had to travel abroad without a passport, and it was the last visit that Green and his wife ever made to Europe. Within a year of their visit to Innsbruck, Britain and Germany were at war; Green was Archdeacon of Monmouth and Lord Merthyr was dead and buried at Aberdare less than a year after the terrible mining disaster at his colliery at Senghenydd. As for Queen Victoria, so for Lord Merthyr, the congregation at St. Elvan's sang "Now the labourer's task is o'er", but this time the nineteenth century had really gone.

1914 in the life of Green, as in the life of the nation, marked a turning-point. In January he was still organising opposition to the Welsh Church Bill and entertaining Bishop John Owen "the great Church defender", and Sir John Sankey at Aberdare. Green's predecessor, Richard Bowen Jenkins, died at Cardigan and Green officiated at his funeral on 9th January. In February Green and his wife were in London for the Lower House of Convocation, the Church's parliament, to which Green had been elected as a proctor by his fellow-clergymen in the Diocese of Llandaff. Green's attendance at Convocation gave him the opportunity of getting to know some of the leading ecclesiastical figures and he was often entertained to lunch at the clubs of leading Llandaff clergymen such as Canon Harding or the new dean, C.E.T. Griffith, the son of one of his predecessors at Aberdare. Mrs. Green accompanied him, and they were able to see something of Green's family. In 1914 they saw Green's youngest sister Edith and his youngest brother Sebald shortly before Sebald took command of the ship in which he was killed in 1919.

On Tuesday 3rd March the Bishop of Llandaff offered Green the Archdeaconry of Monmouth which was accepted by letter on the same day. To the senior archdeaconry of Llandaff the Bishop had appointed James Rice Buckley, the popular Vicar of Llandaff whose canonry of St. Cross in Llandaff Cathedral was then given to H.R. Johnson. Green succeeded William Conybeare Bruce, a former Vicar of St. Woolos,

Newport and a fellow of the Royal Astronomical Society, who had been Archdeacon of Monmouth since 1885.

Green was what was popularly known as a high churchman in an age when such a term excited more bitterness in many high ecclesiastical places than it does to-day. As rural dean of Aberdare, Green had the support, and one suspects the admiration, of Archdeacon Bruce who had lived at Rogiet Rectory since 1901 but was often resident at the canonry on Llandaff Green. Archdeacon Bruce tried to persuade Green to stand as proctor in Convocation for the Archdeaconry of Monmouth in 1910, since he claimed that there were "few incumbents of any light or learning" in the archdeaconry at the time, "and the two or three who whould be eligible are either too young as incumbents or would find the expense of attending Convocation too great a tax". Green sent a telegram in reply to this letter from Bruce, and the telegram of 25th January, 1910 is recorded in red ink in Green's own hand at the bottom of his letter from Bruce. It reads simply: "Quite impossible. The conduct of the last election in spite of protest from my supporters proves that the plan suggested by you is not feasible. Charles Green, Aberdare." Tensions between high and low were strong at that time. One of Green's supporters, the Vicar of Llanbister in Radnorshire, wrote in 1911 to tell Green of his disappointment that Green had not been made Bishop of Llandaff; "I still hope to live long enough to see you one of our Fathers in God. We are in need of one good Catholic out of the four".

Bishop Hughes of Llandaff was not by nature one of Green's supporters. Hughes was low and slow: the cope and mitre were anathema to him. He was one of those bishops who liked to have a mitre on his coat of arms but not on his head.

Archdeacon Bruce recommended that Green should succeed him as Archdeacon of Monmouth when he retired in 1914. Another of Green's supporters, the rector of Dinas Powis, wrote to congratulate him saying that it "really is most encouraging to know that the Bishop can take his courage in both hands and make the best appointment even if he has to set on one side his ecclesiastical inclinations". If we take Archdeacon Bruce seriously, the Bishop of Llandaff had no choice since Green was the only man for the job. Bruce assumed that one of the Monmouth rural deans would have expected to get the job, but Bruce confided to Green his confidence that "the appointment of one of themselves would have left behind it a far more exasperating and lasting sense of soreness" than they would experience at Green's appointment. Bruce went on to say that there was not "one of them whom I could have appointed myself, had I been Bishop, with any feeling but one of profound misgiving".

On Friday 3rd April, 1914, Green was collated by the Bishop and installed by the Dean in Llandaff Cathedral as Archdeacon of Monmouth and Canon of Llangwm. His brother Kenneth, then Vicar of St. Peter Malvern Wells, was there with his mother who was to live for another ten years to see her eldest son become a bishop. Green formally resigned from the living of Aberdare on 25th April, 1914 and his resignation became effective on 1st May.

In the meantime Green held his first induction service as Archdeacon of Monmouth when he inducted the Revd. H. Morice Jones into the Parish Church of Llanfoist, near Abergavenny, on 24th April. By a strange coincidence one of the last things that Green did as archdeacon was to induct the same incumbent into the Parish Church of Llanellen after that Parish had been united with Llanfoist in 1921.

After the induction service at Llanfoist, Green had to return to Aberdare, a journey of two-and-three-quarter hours. He had already decided to live in his archdeaçonry, but he did not become the incumbent of a parish because that would have detracted from the time that he could devote to the affairs of the archdeaconry and the problems that confronted the Church in Wales in the face of impending disestablishment. Green was able to live in the archdeaconry because his wife bought a house in Stow Park Circle in Newport, then known as Stow Park Circus. Mrs. Green paid £3,750 for the house, called Jesmond, which became hers on 30th June, 1914. An imposing mansion, Jesmond was still standing on the junction of Stow Park Circle and Caeperllan Road in the Parish of St. Woolos in 1970, but it has since been razed. To Archdeacon Bruce, Green confided his concern about the attitude of the Newport clergy towards his move and he hoped that the clergy would not think that he wanted to dominate them. But Bruce had no misgivings about the move: "you cannot fail to dominate them" he wrote, "and very much for their good. That is just what they need . . . Newport ecclesiastically sorely needs a heart, to give it some sort of cohesion-you will very soon realise the position there".

Green was warmly received in the archdeaconry. Of the 207 letters and telegrams which he received on his appointment, none was more sincere than that from the rector of Llanhilleth, Daniel Felix. Felix stated that most of the clergy in Monmouthshire were "what might be called moderate Churchmen", and he went on, "I am one of the Evangelical school. There are only a few here of your own school of thought. Yet I feel sure that you will be accorded a hearty welcome to the Archdeaconry". Daniel Felix was rector of Llanhilleth for many years. He became rural dean of Blaenau Gwent in 1916 and he enjoyed a long association with Green throughout which the two men remained on very good terms, although in churchmanship they were poles apart. When Green was translated to Bangor, Felix wrote from Llanhilleth to congratulate him and to offer him hospitality whenever he was in Monmouthshire.

Green enjoyed being an archdeacon and he seemed to revel in the work. He began holding visitations of Churchwardens in various centres in the archdeaconry as soon as he had resigned the living of Aberdare. Green had a very clear mind for legal matters and constitutional issues and no question was put to him without receiving his fullest attention: he always gave a clear and concise answer which he then preserved in his letter-books. At his visitations he quickly detected abuses and his experience as a parish priest enabled him to be strict but fair. The carbon copies of the letters that he sent out as archdeacon reveal his clarity of mind as well as his loyalty to his fellow-clergymen and also to the churchwardens and to the discipline which he had to enforce. To one vicar who was in dispute with the local Company that had given the parish its Parish church, Green wrote that he refused to be used as a vehicle for the expression of the vicar's views to the Company over the lease of the church hall. He reminded the same vicar of his obligations in the matter of the money that the vicar had collected for the churchwardens' funds, and he was not afraid to tell the vicar that he could be prosecuted for the misappropriation of eleemosynary money. Furthermore Green reminded both churchwardens that they were responsible for the administration of the money and that the fund should not be administered at the discretion of only one of them. Green then wrote to the Company to tell them that it was his duty as archdeacon to enquire into all aspects of parochial affairs and that the dispute in which they were involved over the lease of the church hall merely hindered church work. He wrote again to the vicar and urged him in future to administer the hall with the help of a committee. Green's leadership was effective because it was thorough and impartial and he never dodged the issues.

The Great War began on 4th August, 1914. Two days later on the feast of the Transfiguration, Green and his wife moved into Jesmond. The Hon. Mrs. Green liked Jesmond so much that she and her husband remained there until Green became Bishop of Bangor in 1928. They never moved into Bishopstow which became available as the official residence of the Bishop of Monmouth. On Friday 18th September at 12 noon the Welsh Church Act received the Royal assent almost exactly one year after Green's return from that distant holiday in Innsbruck. It had been one of the longest years in Green's life.

Was it academic detachment or a realisation that as far as possible life had to continue on a day-to-day basis that caused Green to spend so much time during the Great War undertaking intensive tours of inspection of the churches in his archdeaconry? He visited the clergymen of the archdeaconry and he preached in their churches every Sunday when he was not on business in London or on holiday. Holidays at this time were spent in Devon or in Scotland. Green still made his confessions to Fr. Ives at St. German's in Cardiff and he went on retreats with the Cowley Fathers in Oxford. He met regularly with the rural deans in his archdeaconry and he appointed T.B.R. Wilson, a Newport solicitor, to be his Registrar in February 1917. His diaries at this time refer frequently to his study of the French Modernist Biblical scholar Alfred Loisy and especially to Loisy's *Le Quatrieme Evangile*, published in 1903, which the Roman Catholic Church had immediately placed upon the Index of prohibited books. Perhaps Loisy was to Green what Hans Kung is to modern Anglicans except that Green read his heretic in the language in which he wrote. By 1917 Loisy had been excommunicated by the Roman Church and had abandoned his priestly functions. Like Hans Kung, Loisy had more in common with some Anglican theologians than with the official Roman teaching of his day.

Green also studied Loisy's more important work *Les Evangiles Synoptiques*, published in 1908, and his copy was bequeathed to St. Michael's College Library. During these years Green also bought fifteen of the eighteen volumes that he bequeathed to St. Michael's College of Hefele's *Histoire des Conciles*, the History of the ecclesiastical councils in a French translation with additions by H. Leclercq, the Benedictine scholar. Green could only afford these expensive volumes through his wife's generosity. She gave him £30 in April 1918, half of which he immediately spent on a book-case from her old home, the Mardy at Aberdare. He could not resist the purchase of a codex of Canon Law and a copy of the directory of modern ceremonial practice produced by the Roman Catholic liturgical writer Adrian Fortescue in 1918 under the title *The Ceremonies of the Roman Rite*.

The Convocation of Canterbury continued to meet throughout the war and to discuss matters that were largely liturgical and unlikely to have affected the disestablished Church in Wales very much. Green attended the meetings and he made one significant intervention in a debate that revealed an aspect of his character that remained consistent throughout his life. To a proposal by two future Archbishops, C.F. Garbett and William Temple in April 1918 that the Church should support the demands of labour for a national minimum wage, for state provision against unemployment, and for a recognition of the status of workers in the industries in which they are engaged, Green proposed an amendment that for the word "support" should be substituted the words, "urge the high court of Parliament to a serious and impartial consideration of". Green said that it was no business of Convocation to tell parliament what acts they should pass. In this amendment Green was well supported by the old Evangelical Dean of Canterbury, Henry Wace and by Canon T.J. Jones of Llandaff, but the amendment was heavily defeated. Green never approved of clergymen, even if they were bishops, interfering in industrial disputes. He always remained deeply conservative about the part that the Church should play in the affairs of the world. He consistently maintained that the Church's intervention in industrial and social affairs merely exacerbated the situation and did the Church no good. Twenty-five years later, when he was Archbishop of Wales, Green told the Governing Body that its primary obligation was "to present Christ Jesus as the Saviour of the World", but Charles Green sometimes acted as if he believed that Christ Jesus was first and foremost the Saviour of the Church.

The Suspensory Act of 1914 suspended the disestablishment of the Welsh Church until the war was over, but it did not suspend the need to prepare for the situation in which the Church in Wales would find itself when the war ended. The Representative Body had to be created to receive property on the date of disestablishment and many other big questions remained unanswered and as uncertain as the date when the war would end. Efforts were made to modify the Welsh Church Act and the Suspensory Act, but these came to nothing and at the same time the Church had to pursue the seemingly contradictory course of preparing for an eventuality that Churchpeople were still fighting to avoid. The joint-committee of the four dioceses of the Church in Wales decided to create a Representative Body to hold and administer the property that would be returned to the Church in Wales by the Welsh Church Commissioners, and the Committee also decided that a Governing Body should be set up to exercise general legislative and administrative authority in the Church. The recommendations of the joint-committee were submitted to the Convention that was held in Cardiff in October 1917 with plenary powers conferred upon it by the Diocesan Conferences. Bishop Edwards of St. Asaph presided but the chief speaker was Mr. Justice Sankey. The Convention marked the beginning of the acceptance of disestablishment as a fact of life for the Church in Wales which then became its official title. The Governing Body and the Representative Body were born and held their first meetings in January 1918.

After the war, the Amending Act of 1919 extended the date of disestablishment to 31st March, 1920. Strange though it may seem, as late as January 1920. the Welsh dioceses did not know whether they would have to withdraw from the Convocation of Canterbury or whether they would be able to elect their own archbishop. The Archbishop of Canterbury advised the Church in Wales to form itself into a new province and he had already indicated to Bishops Edwards and Owen that he would not interfere in the election of the first Archbishop of Wales. Apart from the two bishops, no-one else at the Governing Body meeting at Rhyl in January 1920 seemed to know for certain what was going to happen until Bishop Owen was forced by a question from Archdeacon Green to reveal the facts. That meeting at Rhyl also confirmed the decision to establish the new province of Wales as had been resolved at the meeting of the Governing Body at Llandrindod Wells in June 1919. At that meeting there had been considerable opposition from the diocese of Bangor to the creation of a separate province because the Bishop of Bangor still hoped that the Welsh Church Act would be repealed. In fact, by 1920 no-one seriously believed that disestablishment could be undone and not even the Tory leadership would undertake to try. The best that could be expected was that disendowment might be brought about on terms that were slightly more generous to the Church than had previously seemed likely.

Green's scholarly advice had often been sought by the Bishops during the anxious days of the war when so many issues were uncertain. Could the Act ever be repealed? Was the Church in Wales accepting the inevitable and making repeal less likely by preparing for an orderly transfer of property and administration? When would the war end and so hasten the provisions of the Act? Three areas were of particular concern to Green: these were the exercise of ecclesiastical patronage and the question of who would be responsible for appointing rectors and vicars to the parishes of Wales now that the patronage of the Crown and all other private patronage had ceased? What had happened to the parson's freehold or right to remain in his rectory or vicarage for as long as he lived? The question of the franchise qualification for members of Church bodies also concerned him at all levels from that of the Governing and Representative Bodies to the Diocesan Conference and the Parochial Church Councils. Should women be admitted to membership of all or any of these councils of the Church on the same terms as men? What concerned Green above all during these years was the place of the bishops in the disestablished Church. His consistency and honesty in this matter must be admired all the more because he was not a bishop at the time and he was not therefore safeguarding his vested interests. There seemed little to suggest that he would shortly be elevated to the bench when he first spoke out against any attempt to undermine the Order of bishops in the disestablished Church. Episcopacy was the key to Catholic Order and unless this were preserved inviolate, Green would have nothing to do with the disestablished Church but would, as he told the Cardiff Convention in 1917, "take up his hat and go" if the proposal of Mr. Lovat Fraser, a Llandaff layman, to prohibit the bishops from voting as a separate Order in the Governing Body, had been carried.

"A very able and level-headed man" was the verdict of Bishop John Owen upon Green in September 1914 when Green attended the funeral of Archdeacon Owen Evans at Abergwili and remained behind afterwards to discuss problems with Bishop Owen, Dean Roberts of Bangor and Mr. Frank Morgan, a don at Keble College who later became the first Secretary of the Representative and Governing Bodies of the Church in Wales.

In 1915 Green was not entirely in favour of the creation of a Governing Body of the Church in Wales because he thought it would undermine the authority of the Provincial Synod of the Welsh bishops and it might usurp their peculiar rights. Green issued two privately printed memoranda in March and April 1915. In the first Green stated that the bishops and clergy of the Church in Wales were excluded from the Convocation of Canterbury by the Welsh Church Act. He respectfully suggested that the Archbishop of Canterbury should inform the Church in Wales of his intentions. If the Welsh bishops and clergy were not summoned to Convocation, then that body ceased to be a valid Provincial Synod of Canterbury as it was then constituted. If the Archbishop of Canterbury ignored the Welsh Church Act and summoned the Welsh bishops and clergy, then the Synod would have no validity in the State's eyes and no new synod set up by the Archbishop could alter the fact that the Convocation remained the constitutional body in the eyes of the law for enacting canons. Green thought that the proposed Governing Body of the Church in Wales would have limited legislative and regulative authority, but it would not be a Provincial Synod although it would affect the authority and rights of the bishops. "It is unseemly", he wrote, "that any assembly should deal with such points (concerning patronage and appointments to vacant sees; diocesan and parochial boundaries; cathedral chapters and changes in ecclesiastical law and courts) except a Provincial Synod". Green thought that the Archbishop and Convocation might be asked to begin the setting up of a separate Province for Wales before the date of disestablishment.

Archdeacon Green's second memorandum of 12th April, 1915 urged that the Governing Body would not be an ecclesiastical Synod and therefore any scheme of patronage or nomination devised by the Governing Body would operate only by the favour of each individual bishop "unless it received Canonical authority from the Provincial Synod or Convocation of Canterbury before the date of disestablishment". Green went on to argue that a Governing Body that was not a Provincial Synod could not alter ecclesiastical law, except in those particulars which could be traced to a parliamentary origin. He believed that the Governing Body should be subordinated to the Provincial Synod of Canterbury, or else it should "retire in favour of the Provincial Synod of Wales".

The schemes for the Representative Body and the Governing Body went ahead in spite of the Bishop of Bangor's fears that the Welsh Church Act would not be repealed once the Governing Body was set up. The Representative Body had to be set up to receive the temporalities from the Welsh Church Commissioners when disestablishment came into effect. Archdeacon Green wanted the Representative Body to be controlled by the Synod but, according to Miss Eluned Owen, "both Mr. Frank Morgan and the Bishop (Owen) had come to the conclusion that the right solution was to set up a Welsh Council but not a Welsh Synod". The formation of a Synod, as they realised, would cut the Church in Wales off from the Province of

Canterbury in a way which a Governing Body would not. Green also realised this, but to his question, "What is gained by the delay?" he received no answer. The Welsh Bishops and clergy were excluded from the Convocation of Canterbury by the Welsh Church Act. Green saw no reason why the Church in Wales should not accept the fact and make provision for a Synod that would have the necessary episcopal authority to carry out the work of the new province. Bishop Owen continued to argue that "if the little group headed by Archdeacon Green had their way, Welsh Churchmen might themselves, by their own actions, make it impossible to repeal dismemberment - the forcible severance of the Church in Wales from the Church in England".[9]

Events were to prove that Green had been right all along. The Welsh Church Act might have left the Church in Wales within the Province of Canterbury but the Welsh bishops soon had to face the fact that their exclusion from its Synod gave them no alternative but to accept from Archbishop Davidson the advice that they would not accept from Archdeacon Green and proceed to the creation of a separate province. At the meeting of the Governing Body at Rhyl in January 1920, confirming the decision to set up a separate province of the Church in Wales, Green's point about the protection of episcopal authority by the creation of a provincial Synod was safeguarded. Lord Justice Bankes, on behalf of the constitutional committee, proposed that the best solution of the difficulty over the provincial Synod would be the addition of clauses to the constitution of the Governing Body explaining that the diocesan bishops sit in the Governing Body as representatives of the ancient provincial Synod and that nothing in the constitution shall interfere with their authority as such, except that the right of legislation is reserved to the Governing Body in accordance with the methods laid down in the constitution. The Bishops also retained their right to meet separately from the Governing Body with the suffragan and assistant bishops present for consultation purposes but without a vote. In seconding this recommendation, Archdeacon Green stated clearly his belief that it must be at all times clear that the final voice in the Church must remain with the diocesan bishops ". . . who constituted the ancient Provincial Synod as the core of the whole Church assembly".

"The Archdeacon put the whole matter in its historical setting" is the verdict of Bishop Owen's biographer about Green's contribution to the Cardiff Convention in 1917. Of Green's part in the meeting of the Governing Body at Cardiff in September 1918, Bishop Owen wrote to Archbishop Davidson to say that Archdeacon Green "who is a weighty authority on Canon Law" was "exceedingly valuable to us".[10] At that meeting Green had spoken mainly of the problem of fixity of tenure in relation to Church appointment in Wales. According to one proposed amendment to clause 35 of the new constitution, a lesser tribunal would be set up to investigate cases concerning unsuitable incumbents in parishes. Green said that the proposer of the amendment made a "grievous slip when he would give the tribunal the power of deprivation which, surely, belongs to the bishop". Of other proposed amendments to the same clause, Archdeacon Green said that "in the intricate question of the benefice, I am not sure that the bishops can be told by you to institute on the conditions which you may choose to lay down; I mean at this stage of your existence". Green concluded that the Governing Body might control the temporalities of a benefice and even deprive a clergyman of his income, but that would not deprive him of his spiritual office "and you cannot at present (as I have shown) by your resolutions, determine the spiritual acts of the bishops".

That was on 26th September, 1918. The armistice in the Great War took place on 11th November. Green continued with his work in the archdeaconry and with his scholarly pursuits. He spent his wife's Christmas gift of five pounds in joining the London Library. Archdeacon Bruce died in February 1919 and Green officiated at his funeral. That spring, Green prepared for his vernal visitation of the archdeaconry as he had during every spring throughout the war. Appropriately that year the theme of his charge to the clergy and churchwardens was "Peace and Unity".

Green began his charge, delivered during May 1919, with thanksgiving to God for "our safe deliverance from the most terrific war which the world has known". He referred to the creation of the League of Nations on 28th April, of which he said: "I fervently hope that the clergy and laity of the Church — the Church which throughout the Middle Ages never ceased to dream of a Holy Empire which should control the selfishness of the nations — will keep the vision of the league before the people, temper the criticisms which may be directed against it, and work, so far as in them lies, for its speedy realisation". Green saw the implications of all this for the Christian Church. Improved communication between nations brought much greater contact of the "backward races" with the "civilisation of the leading nations". There was therefore, thought Green, a need for "a great expansion of Christian missions". What he called "the evils of a divided Christendom" were also more apparent, he said, in an age when it was no longer easy for each Christian denomination to have its "zone of influence" in the mission field. Converts were confused by the varieties of interpretations and disciplines that they encountered through their increasing contact with more than one denominational version of Christianity. Was organic reunion of the Christian denominations possible, asked Green, "in order to win mankind completely for Christ"?

While the League of Nations should encourage the denominations in their determination to unite, and some progress had already been made within the Anglican Church, Green believed that premature action by individuals or sections of denominations would hinder rather than help the progress towards reunion. He quoted a leading Nonconformist who deprecated a mere exchange of pulpits between the denominations. "We must discover that we are agreed" said Green, "before we act as if we were". He quoted the late Bishop Stubbs of Oxford in support of his very conservative view of how little participation there could be between Church and Nonconformity. Bishop Stubbs had died in 1901 but it was still only 1919 and the wounds of disestablishment in Wales were still raw.

Green did not mention disestablishment in his charge, but he kept to his lofty theme of the need for greater unity throughout Christendom and what was achieved "for the benefit of the human race" of "even a divided Christendom". He claimed that it was not the Church that had failed in Germany where "the language of heathen Prussia" had prevailed; nor in Russia where "the Church is permitted to have but one service a week, and worshippers are compelled to pay more than double the theatre tax", nor even in Britain where he claimed that there was "an indication that 'the animal soul of the past' is reasserting itself in our generation". The fact that the Church "still abides, and comes out victorious, is evidence of her divine origin". Green concluded that the League of Nations would not have been possible without the Church because the mutual trust on which all international communion relies came from Christianity.

It would be easy to criticise the charge or to caricature it as advocating Christian reunion for the benefit of "the heathen in his blindness" but not good enough for the "civilisation of the leading nations" who appreciated the difference between Church and Dissent. Such a censure would be anachronistic. The charge dealt positively with the real achievements that then seemed possible through the League of Nations. It reminded its hearers of the fact of original sin even if it was a little unrealistic about the indefectibility of the Church. At least the charge realistically faced the situation in which its listeners found themselves in 1919.

That August, while he was on holiday in Devon, Green heard the news of the explosion which destroyed H.M.S. Glowworm at Beresnik on the river Dvina. The ship, commanded by his youngest brother Sebald, was taking supplies to the White army in Russia in the fight against the Red army in the last-ditch attempt to overthrow the revolutionary forces. Sebald, aged thirty-nine, was the baby of the family and he had never married. Green was clearly upset by his death although two other brothers, Wilfrith and Sebert had both returned safely from war- service.

Green was in residence at Llandaff during the first three months of 1920. He continued to attend the meetings of Convocation in London.

He was still a member of Convocation, for the time being, and he thought it essential that the links between the Church of England and the Church in Wales should be retained in spite of ecclesiastical separation. To attendance at Convocation were now added the meetings of the Representative and Governing Bodies, and the Rhyl meeting of the Governing Body in January 1920, confirmed the decision to set up the new province of the Church in Wales. Archbishop Davidson formally released the Welsh Bishops from their oaths of allegiance to him as their Metropolitan and he told Convocation on 10th February that the four Welsh dioceses were free to form themselves into a Province.

On 6th April, 1920, Easter Tuesday, Green left for Llandrindod Wells where he acted as Chaplain to the Bishop of Llandaff at the Holy Communion service and election of the first Archbishop of Wales in the old parish church at Llandrindod on Wednesday 7th April. At the Governing Body meeting at Llandrindod on Friday 9th, Green moved the official welcome to Alfred George Edwards the first Archbishop, and he attended the confirmation of the election of the Archbishop by the diocesan bishops in Holy Trinity church during Friday morning. The Welsh Bishops issued their mandate for the enthronement of the Archbishop at St. Asaph on Tuesday 1st June.

The enthronement of the senior Welsh Bishop, Edwards of St. Asaph, as Archbishop of Wales has been described by him in his *Memories* as a national festival, and by his lieutenant, Bishop Owen, as "a festival of national sentiment". Green was the liturgical authority to whom everyone deferred in the compiling of the order of service that was used. The service began with the hymn, the Old Hundredth, and went on with the bidding prayer, the Lord's Prayer and the Apostles' Creed. The Archbishop of Canterbury preached the sermon and then the Bishop of London read the necessary legal documents. After that, the Archbishop-elect, vested in a cope, faced the congregation from the sanctuary and made the oath on an original copy of William Salesbury's New Testament of 1567. The Archbishop of Canterbury then enthroned the Archbishop and handed to him the archiepiscopal cross. The new archbishop put on his mitre to receive the oaths of allegiance of his suffragans.

After the *Te Deum* and Litany and the blessing by the Archbishop of Wales, the procession of Archbishops left the cathedral to the singing of the Welsh tune Hyfrydol. There followed the presentation of the Archbishop to his people by the Archbishop of Canterbury. Speeches were made in Welsh and English and everyone joined in saying the Lord's Prayer. The Archbishop of Wales gave the blessing and the presentation concluded with the singing of the Welsh National Anthem.

Prince Arthur of Connaught had represented the King because the Prince of Wales was overseas. Lloyd George had gone with great enthusiasm and had embarrassed everyone by making his communion at the early morning service before the enthronement. Green retained a customary discreet silence about this prominent Nonconformist presenting himself for communion, but he seems more concerned that the timing of the enthronement was right. The service had started at 11.30 a.m. and was over by 12.45 p.m. If there had been rather more recital of legal documents than one might have expected in such a service, then Green must take the blame. More than a thousand people attended the luncheon in a marquee afterwards with Prince Arthur and Lloyd George. The best possible solution to the battle over disestablishment had been found and the independent Province of Wales was left to organise its own affairs for the future. The place of Charles Green in the life of that province was already guaranteed. Both as a canon lawyer and as a liturgiologist, he was already beginning to make himself indispensable.

5. Bishop of Monmouth

After the first world war when disestablishment became a reality, Green was preoccupied with preparations for the independent government of the Province of Wales. He had just the right mind for the niceties of ecclesiastical law that was required at the time, and he collaborated with the learned Mr. Justice Sankey and Mr. Frank Morgan in the framing of the Constitution. Many years later, after the publication of Green's book on the Constitution, Sankey wrote to congratulate Green and said that had he realised when he drafted the new constitution that there was such a mass of learning behind it, and that there was a man who knew it all, "I am afraid I should have feared to rush in".

In June 1921 Green stayed with Mr. Justice Sankey at 14, Deans Yard where they worked at the draft of the new constitution together with Frank Morgan until after eleven o'clock at night on two successive days. In July Green was correcting the proofs of the new edition of the constitution.

At the beginning of 1921, preparations were under way for the creation of the new diocese of Monmouth, but they had to be made before it was known who the new bishop would be. It was thought that the old diocese of St. David's might be divided before that of Llandaff, though the Bishop of St. David's was opposing the division of his own diocese and he was also opposing the division of the Llandaff diocese, because he thought that the division of the latter would further strengthen the move to divide the former. Furthermore it was not known whether Joshua Pritchard Hughes would remain at Llandaff as bishop or would come to Monmouth as its first bishop and leave Llandaff vacant. Bishop Hughes was then seventy-four. He was dissatisfied with his house at Llandaff and had said that if a good enough house and salary were provided at Monmouth he might move.

Faced with intransigent bishops, the new Secretary of the Representative Body, Frank Morgan, wrote to Green from 39, Cathedral Road, to say that Green was one of the few who realised what had yet to be done, and Morgan listed the following necessities:- division of dioceses, amalgamation of benefices, a central examination for ordinands, a clergy superannuation scheme, tribunals and the problem of episcopal palaces. "All these" Morgan concluded solemnly, "are important and need thought and consideration".

Green had already heard from another prominent layman, Sir Henry Mather Jackson, on the question of the division of the old diocese of Llandaff. In October 1920, a commission of which Green was chairman, had proposed that the new diocese should be called Monmouth. Jackson wanted it to be called the Diocese of Caerleon or failing that, Gwent. He strongly protested against the name "Caerleon and Newport", which he must have heard had been considered, but he said that he was glad to see that Brynmawr was included in the new diocese. He must have been very disappointed when Brynmawr was left out.

Jackson and Lord Tredegar played a big part in the preparations for the new diocese that were made at this time, with the Archbishop of Wales keeping a fatherly eye on the proceedings. The Archbishop asked T.B.R. Wilson to persuade Lord Tredegar to preside over a county meeting to raise funds for the bishopric, but Jackson was opposed to this too, since he thought that what could be raised by such a meeting could be raised anyway. The Bishop of Llandaff remained the great unknown quantity. It was not known what proportion of his stipend he would be prepared to contribute towards the new bishop. When Lord Tredegar gave his house, King's Hill, to the Representative Body for the new bishop, Jackson expressed the hope that it would not be called a palace.

In addition to the house in Newport, built on land that was originally known as Molly Rosser's farm and later to become Bishopstow, Lord Tredegar gave £500 a year for three years towards the Bishop's stipend. With the promise of £310 from the Representative Body and subsequently of £100 from the Archbishop, plans were made for a visit from the Archbishop who would meet leading laymen invited by Lord Tredegar, in the hope of raising the balance of £1090 to make up the salary to £2,000 a year.

This was the position in April 1921, and it was probably the proposed visit of the Archbishop about which Green was in correspondence with him in June, Archbishop Edwards wrote briefly from St. Asaph to thank Green for offering to provide him with a cope and mitre but he said that he only used them for ordinations and consecrations and on the great festivals: "I am afraid", he concluded, "I do not wish at present to depart from the general rule".

By the beginning of September 1921, Morgan could report that T.B.R. Wilson had secured promises of contributions towards the bishop's salary totalling £1,900, and there were still several prominent Monmouthshire people who had not yet answered the appeal. Morgan asked Green whether it would be possible to reduce the stipend to £2,000 a year with the house after three years, if £2,200 could be obtained at the beginning together with the £310 from the Representative Body.

But the position of the proposed new diocese was by no means secure at this late date and less than a week before its creation, Frank Morgan was still not optimistic about the outcome. There was opposition from many quarters because the bishop's salary had to be raised by voluntary contribution and was guaranteed for only three years. The obvious question was asked by many: what would happen at the end of the three years? Morgan reported to Green that Sir Owen Phillips thought it very undignified to raise a bishop's salary by voluntary contributions, and Morgan was certain that the St. David's contingent would try to block Monmouth because of the uncertainty about its future. "I would prefer open opposition" concluded Morgan, "as it is easier to meet, but I still hope to see a new bishop this year".

In spite of the opposition and the failure to secure the division of St. David's diocese, plans had gone ahead. There were other problems associated with the proposed new see apart from the bishop's house and salary. Frank Morgan had considered the arms of the new diocese, and he wrote to Green endorsing the opinion of the Herald of the College of Arms that the seals of Newport and Monmouth Boroughs should be embodied in the arms of the new see. The name of the see remained unknown, and Morgan was afraid of the criticism that would ensue if the matter were prejudged by getting a design for arms. Frank Morgan advised Green to ask the Herald to prepare a design embodying what suggestions he thought right, and Morgan thought that this should be submitted to the new bishop, and if he approved it, the seal could be cut while the Herald was granting the arms. Morgan himself personally guaranteed the fee for the arms, but hesitated to act officially before the Representative Body had affirmed the creation of the new see.

The creation of the new diocese was decreed by the Governing Body at Llandrindod Wells on 29th September 1921, and the territory it comprised ceased to be part of the diocese of Llandaff on 18th October. Archdeacon Green had clearly established himself as the obvious choice as first bishop of the new diocese of Monmouth, and he was elected to that office in St. Woolos on 18th November when, as the Western Mail photograph shows, the doors were guarded by a policeman. Green received twenty-six of the thirty-three votes. Only two of the three clergymen who had been elected to represent the Diocese of Bangor were present. The Electoral College comprised the Archbishop and the three diocesan bishops of the Church in Wales; six electors, three clerical and three lay, from the dioceses of St. Asaph and St. David's; five electors from the diocese of Bangor and twelve, six clerical and six lay from the diocese of Llandaff. At that time the Diocese of Monmouth had no Diocesan Conference to appoint its electors and therefore no official representatives at the election of its first bishop. The bishop's stipend may have been raised in a manner analogous to the payment of the local nonconformist minister, but the method of his appointment was very different. The only clergyman resident within the new diocese who had a vote in the election was Archdeacon Green himself and only two lay voters, Sir Henry Mather Jackson and Leolin Forestier Walker, lived in the diocese. Had the college not completed its business within three days, the right of appointment would have gone to the Archbishop of Canterbury, but the college took only one and a half hours to reach its decision and Green returned to Jesmond for lunch at 12 noon with Dr. Joyce, then principal of St. David's College, Lampeter and later to succeed Green as Bishop, and Mr. Frank Morgan who had been the secretary of the electoral college.

Green was consecrated bishop on 21st December at Llandaff Cathedral and he was enthroned in the pro-Cathedral of St. Woolos, Newport on 3rd January, 1922. In the meantime he had appointed T.B.R. Wilson to be the first Registrar of the diocese, and Wilson had undertaken to reserve a large room in his offices "in which you have several times sat for special business" as the registry, "and to place an able and reliable clerk in sole charge under me". Wilson had been suggested as a possible chancellor for the new diocese, but Green had some doubts about Wilson's qualifications to act as chancellor, and it is evidence of Green's thoroughness that he secured through Sankey the opinions of two legal experts, Phillimore and Parmoor, on the subject, and he carefully preserved their replies. Parmoor thought that the solicitor (Wilson) if he were over the age of thirty and qualified to be a member of the Governing Body, was qualified to be a chancellor. Phillimore replied that he had no objection to a solicitor being chancellor, though if it were in England where the chancellor had judicial functions because of Establishment, "I should hesitate before advising the appointment of a solicitor". Wilson did not however become chancellor: the job was given to a barrister, Wilfred Herbert Poyer Lewis, later to become a High Court judge.

The day after Green was elected bishop, the Warden of his old college, the Revd Dr. B.J. Kidd, wrote to congratulate him and ended his letter : "We know now that there is at least *one* Catholic Bishop in Wales, and that he is what he is by free canonical election". Four days later, Kidd wrote again to recommend Archibald Frederic Hood to Green as an examining chaplain. The day before, another old Keble friend, Frank Morgan, had recommended the Latin form of Monmouth - *Monemutensis*, abbreviated to Monemuten., as the most suitable title for the bishop, and this was duly heeded by Green as was Kidd's recommendation of Frederic Hood.

It was fitting that the first occasion on which Bishop Green administered the rite of Confirmation was in the parish church of St. John the Baptist on Risca Road, Newport on 9th February, 1922. The parish was in the Tractarian tradition. It is a small parish that had been part of St. Woolos parish until 1898, when Archdeacon Bruce's curate at St. Woolos, James Francis Summers, became its first vicar. Green liked to worship at St. John's and he regularly went there when he was archdeacon if he was not needed elsewhere. As recently as ten years ago, several old people in that part of Newport could remember Green walking regularly from his house in Stow Park Circle to St. John's church with a parasol held erect on sunny days. He engaged no-one in conversation *en route* and he refused to make appointments with anyone while he was walking to church. The communicants of St. John Baptist church presented Green with a mitre on Saturday 15th April, 1922 which he wore at what he called a Pontifical High Celebration of Holy Eucharist at the church on the following day which was Easter.

In one sense Green was fortunate that his unique position as the first bishop of a diocese without a proper cathedral or cathedral chapter gave him greater choice about where he went to church than might otherwise have been so, but he did not neglect the pro-Cathedral of St. Woolos where the parishioners had provided him with his throne, and he preached there at Evensong on Easter Day. Green's former assistant curates at Aberdare presented him with a chasuble in May, and the silver pastoral staff and cope of the diocese were presented to him at St. Woolos on 15th September.

The first Monmouth Diocesan Conference was prescribed by paragraph seven of the decree of the Governing Body which created the diocese. The first Conference came into existence with the diocese but it did not meet until summoned by the Bishop. Green's address to the first annual meeting of the second Conference on 12th November, 1923 stated unequivocally his concept of the bishop's authority in his diocese as the one only source of ecclesiastical mission and jurisdiction. The bishop alone, said Green, "is the channel through whom our Blessed Lord, the Head of the Church, confers authority externally to act in his name in this portion of his vineyard...and as the bishop has bestowed, so he has the right to enquire whether the powers which he has entrusted to others are being used as they were meant to be used, according to the mind and intention of the Church at large". "Therefore" Green continued. "the Bishop is the Visitor of the diocese par excellence", and he went on to announce his Primary Visitation of the diocese in May 1924.

In spite of his long-cherished high views of episcopacy, Green did not act in stubborn independence of his advisers and fellow clergy. His letters reveal a man who knew where to get the best advice and knew how to take it when it was given. Older clergymen were frequently impressed by the humility with which he would ask them whom they thought would be most suitable to succeed them on their retirement. Green had been a parish priest himself for twenty-six years, and he was always jealous of the right of the incumbent in his own parish. His address to the second Diocesan Conference contained also the words, "parochial rights strictly speaking refer to an incumbent", a principle of importance to Green and enshrined in the Constitution. He had been an archdeacon for seven years, and he knew the importance of the *oculus episcopi* whose watchful eye might not report everything to the bishop, but would see that the bishop's policy was observed. Green had also been a rural dean and he had written a learned pamphlet on that office for which, as one would expect, he had studied the classic work in no less than two volumes, published in 1835.

William Dansey's *Horae Decanicae Rurales* inspired Green to launch into the subject of the rural deanery in his primary Visitation charge in May 1924. Green was concerned because the rural deaneries of the new diocese were too large. A scheme had been drawn up in 1922 to increase the number of rural deaneries in the hope that they would then be more effective units of administration. Green drily recounted the history of the rural deaneries in the diocese, recalling that the four ancient deaneries of Abergavenny, Usk, Netherwent and Newport had remained unchanged for more than six hundred years. Until the nineteenth century, the only change that he had observed, said Green, was that Kemeys Commander passed from Abergavenny Deanery to that of Usk between 1254 and 1535. The Newport deanery alone stretched from the River Usk to the Rhymney and northwards to Bedwellty. The deaneries of Netherwent, Usk and Abergavenny had been subdivided in 1825 and 1875 when the deanery of Blaenau Gwent was created, followed by those of Raglan, Monmouth and Caerleon twenty years later. Green recommended that Caerleon deanery be suppressed, and he praised the magnanimity of the rural dean who resigned to make this possible and was rewarded for his pains by becoming the first rural dean of the new deanery of Pontypool. A further deanery was established at Bassaleg. Green thought that the Scheme of September 1922 would prove acceptable to all who had the vision to look beyond their own parishes.

As well as creating more rural deaneries in the interests of efficiency and the collection of the new Quota, Green was concerned with the need to create more parishes in the heavily populated industrial areas of the diocese. Between 1st April, 1920 and 18th October, 1921, the Representative Body provided money for seven new parishes at Abercarn, Blackwood, Newbridge, Crumlin, Garndiffaith, and St. Julian's and St. Stephen's in Newport. The parish of St. Andrew's, Liswerry was later added to this list because its creation had been made possible by uniting the parish of Llanelen with that of Llanfoist. In the years 1922-24, the diocese was allowed to create one new parish a year, so that Cwmcarn, Cwmtillery and Victoria each obtained its own incumbent. The parishes of Ynysddu and Six Bells were created in April 1925, facilitated by uniting rural parishes: on the same day that the Vicar of Six Bells was instituted to his cure of souls, the Vicar of Llantilio Crossenny was granted the care of the parishioners of Llanfihangel ystern Llewern.

Green referred to the need for church building in his second Visitation charge in May 1927. He mentioned the consecration of St. Luke's church, Abercarn in 1926 and of St. Julian's Newport in the same year. The foundation stone had been laid at Ynysddu and Green consecrated the church in July 1927. In his short episcopate Green had created a dozen or so parishes and amalgamated several country benefices.

At this point it might be asked what difference Green made to the clergy of the new diocese. When Green became their Father in God, he had already been familiar to them as their archdeacon for seven years. Familiar is hardly the right word. Green was as precise in his personal relationships as in everything else. He agreed to see his clergy only by appointment, and he expected from them correctness of dress and personal behaviour. Himself a prelate of great dignity, he expected his clergy to be mindful of the dignity of their high calling. But there is always the danger of interpreting Green to posterity only as a pompous bore. He was a child of his times and he could have lived in no other, but such a platitude does less than justice to the courtesy and humility testified by those with eyes to penetrate the mask of his shyness. There is no evidence that he was narrowly partisan in his appointments. The theological spectrum of the diocese was broader during his episcopate than it is at present. Perhaps it would be more true to say that the Churchmanship of the whole province was less monochrome in those infant days when the English umbilical cord was newly cut. A number of Green's clergymen could be described as Evangelicals. A lower proportion had received their training in Wales than is now the case.

The decade 1920-1930 was one in which the Anglican Church bemoaned a shortage of clergy from which she did not begin to recover until the early thirties. Only a comparative study of the ordination lists of all the dioceses of England and Wales during this period would show Monmouth in its true light, but Green was not conscious of such a decline in ordinands as a hindrance to his policy of expansion and development. Suffice it to say that fifty more clergy were serving the diocese during Green's episcopate than are there to-day, and the diocese could boast more clergy in the years between 1921 and 1928 than she could in 1930. Moreover, more than half of the forty-one assistant curates listed in the first Diocesan Calendar in 1923 had been licensed to their curacies since 1921.

Between the youngest deacon and the oldest parish priest in 1923, there was a difference in age of more than seventy years, an incredible fact to modern minds. The nonagenarian, Christopher Cook, Vicar of Pontymoel and Rector of Mamhilad, had served the former parish since his ordination in 1850 and the latter since 1855. Cook had the services of an assistant priest at Mamhilad, David Lewis Griffiths, of the comparatively tender age of seventy-one. The Rector of Gwernesney, James Blower, was over eighty, and the Vicar of Malpas, Edward Jenkins, not far behind: both had served their parishes for half a century or more. William Henry Williams (senior) had been Rector of Portskewett since 1880, and the Vicar of Risca, Basil Williams, had served that parish since 1877.

It may seem strange to some that Green was prepared to be the bishop of a diocese that had neither a Cathedral nor a Chapter. Paragraph five of the decree which created the diocese in September 1921, had in fact stated that there should be no Cathedral or Chapter in the diocese until the Governing Body determined otherwise, but it had provided for the parish church of St. Woolos to serve as pro-cathedral. That was the situation which Green accepted when he became bishop, and for his own part he was perfectly satisfied with it. He said as much in his address to the Diocesan Conference in November 1923, but he wanted to know the opinion of Conference on the matter, and he thought that the diocese might be criticised and unfavourably regarded since the more-recently created diocese of Swansea and Brecon already had its cathedral at Brecon. Green had in fact appointed a commission to examine the possibilities of a cathedral in the diocese and various churches, including St. Woolos, together with Chepstow, St. Mary's Abergavenny, Usk and Monmouth had been examined for this purpose, but they had all been rejected, St. Woolos because of its small sanctuary and architectural unsuitability. In May 1926 Green said that St. Woolos was "unquestionably a wonderful old building, a charming parish church". He thought that the diocese should "do nothing in the way of extension to spoil it, and yet, in its present state, it is not at all suitable for use as a cathedral". He emphasised the unsuitability of St. Woolos at that stage because he wanted to strengthen the argument for building an entirely new cathedral, which the Diocesan Conference endorsed in 1927. It was proposed to build the new cathedral on a site of about five acres in a commanding position on Bassaleg Road, Newport, adjacent to the house called Stelvio. In his second Visitation charge in 1927, Green made only slight reference to the cathedral, stating that there seemed to be general agreement that the future cathedral had better be an entirely new edifice.

Green's ideas about cathedral chapters were as strong as his insistence on the importance of the rural dean. In 1923, in the same address to the Diocesan Conference, he said that the phrase "Cathedral and Chapter" excluded the notion, "widespread but errorneous", that the title "canon" was merely honorific involving neither duties nor responsibility. "It is", he went on, "a thing almost unheard of in Christendom for a few clergy to be picked out of a diocese in recognition of their past services and given the title "Canon" without being attached to a chapter. A canonry is bestowed, not as a reward to one whose days of labour are over, but as an opportunity for fresh work, of which the previous work has proved the canon capable". Green also thought it impossible for a parish church to serve as a cathedral, since the parochial rights would, he claimed, interfere with the cathedral and be a "bar to efficiency and a constant ground for friction". For these reasons Green postponed the creation of a cathedral chapter and he bequeathed the problem to his successor, but when the chapter was constituted in 1930, it was decreed that "to not less than five of the canons is to be assigned the supervision and organisation of special departments of Church work in the diocese". Thus far Green had his way.

Green's reign as Bishop of Monmouth had its moments of controversy, not because Green sought controversy but because he was a very strong character with clear and informed opinions about the way in which the affairs of the Church should be conducted and her worship maintained. Green hated anything that was slovenly or untidy in the worship of the Church, and since his time at Aberdare, he had at hand very clear instructions about worship which seemed to cover every contingency. His acquaintances regarded him as a liturgical expert, and there are several letters to Green from the Revd Mark Carpenter-Garnier, requesting Green's advice on points of liturgy and ceremonial when Carpenter-Garnier was about to go to Colombo as Bishop in 1924. When he had been enthroned at Colombo, Carpenter-Garnier wrote to ask Green for a copy of the form of service that he used for the installation of archdeacons, and he begged to know where he should have his throne for a celebration of pontifical High Mass! He went on to ask such questions as whether he should use his mitre when pontifical High Mass was not possible. Carpenter-Garnier had previously requested a copy of Green's diocesan directions about ceremonial which he had found very helpful.

All this has been mentioned to show that Green took great pains in the ordering of services, and of no service was this more true than of the Ordination service. As early as 24th February, 1922 Green had discussed the details of his first Ordination service with his examining chaplains, Frederic Hood and H.J. Riddelsdell, when he had lunch with them at Oxford. On 12th August the Vicar of Christchurch, Newport, E.A. Thorne, drove Green to St. Mary's parish church, Monmouth, "to view it for the purpose of the Ordination". The pastoral staff and cope of the diocese were first used at this ordination. The preacher was Canon C.J. Smith, principal of Ely Theological College and a former sub-warden of St. Michael's College.

Green's Ordination service at Monmouth that September was described in great detail in the *Church Times* and highly praised by Green's friend, Frank Morgan, who found it a "great relief to assist at such a celebration after the dismal and depressing services at Llandaff." Morgan doubted that there had been a similar service in Wales during the last two hundred years. The *Church Times* account was read by that formidable latitudinarian bishop Herbert Hensley Henson of Durham. Henson protested to the *Times* in October at what he called the Use of Monmouth, and he objected to Green's investing the Gospeller with a white silk dalmatic and placing on the priest "a folded chasuble". Henson resented the claim of the *Church Times* that the service had been "most carefully ordered" and "what we have come to expect of the learned prelate (Green)". "The new bishop may be learned" retorted Henson, "but he does not appear to be orderly". Henson then accused Green of acting contrary to the rites and ceremonies of the Church of England, which could not be set aside in Wales except by Bill procedure in the Governing Body. "The principles now called Anglo-Catholic" concluded Henson, "cannot be reconciled with the discipline and doctrine of any Reformed Church and apply as much in a disestablished as an established Church". To this attack Green replied with calm and scholarly brevity two days later. He said simply that by Bill procedure *nemine contradicente* the Governing Body of the Church in Wales made it part of the law of the Church in Wales that the courts of the Church in Wales would not be bound by any decision of the English Courts or of the Judicial Committee of the Privy Council in relation to matters of faith, discipline and ceremonial. "By this deliberate enactment" wrote Green, "the Welsh Church has expressed its intention to interpret the formularies and rules which have been adopted, without regard to any narrow or partisan spirit, which has dominated the interpretation thereof in times past".

Two days later a letter appeared in *The Times* from the Archbishop of Wales, in an apparent panic at the sudden publicity that was being given to the new Province, and stating that the questions raised in Henson's and Green's letters could be "more becomingly decided elsewhere". Green did not write again, but Henson replied to Green's letter in terms which one could only say amounted to incomprehensible gibberish. He said that he could only assume that Green admitted the grave character of his action and claimed that Green had no kind of authority for the deliberate departure from the Ordinal of the Church of England, and that Green apparently claimed the right to create his own Use. Since Green had used the Prayer Book Ordinal at the Ordination at Monmouth, one is left wondering what Henson meant, unless he is in fact doing what Green said that the Church in Wales would not do, having regard for a narrow or partisan spirit. Several laymen jumped in on this correspondence. One, who signed himself a "Welsh Churchman and not a High Churchman", claimed with some justice that when the Welsh Church had appealed for financial assistance the Church of England had left her alone, and the Church of England ought now to be consistent and leave the Church in Wales to deal with matters which concern only herself."[11]

A reading of the Ordinal of 1550, as used in the Church of England at the time of disestablishment, reveals nothing which forbids the use of the dalmatic or the chasuble. True, the Ordinal does not state that there is to be a tradition of these vestments as was provided in the Ordinal of the Pontifical, but the intention of the Reformers in 1550 was to emphasise the essentials of the rite and to leave all else, in the spirit of true Anglicanism, to the realm of things indifferent. In this matter, as in most aspects of ecclesiastical law and administration, the benefit of the doubt would seem to lie with Bishop Green.

In fairness to Green, it should be said that not all his Ordinations were what he called a "solemn celebration of Holy Orders", but he usually managed one of these each year at St. Mary's, Monmouth while he was Bishop of that diocese. He held at least one "low celebration of Holy Orders" every year and two in some years, usually at St. Woolos, Newport, although on 15th May, 1927, Green held an Ordination at St. Mark's church, Newport, when the preacher was E.W. Williamson, the warden of St. Michael's College, Llandaff. At such "low celebrations" the ceremonial was kept to a minimum and the dalmatic and chasuble were not conferred upon the deacon and priest respectively. For these services Green generally employed preachers who might prefer them such as Archdeacon Griffiths, the Vicar of St. Woolos; the Vicar of St. Mark's or the Vicar of St. Paul's or Dr. Corner, his examining chaplain for licensed readers. At Monmouth the preachers were drawn from farther afield, such as Dr. Kidd of Keble (1923); Dr. Joyce (1924) or Archdeacon Prosser of St. David's (1925).

Some people have accused Green of reviving the obsolete practice of episcopal visitations in the Church in Wales. Green certainly conducted two visitations in the Diocese of Monmouth in 1924 and 1927 and he continued the practice when he was translated to Bangor. At neither of his visitations of Monmouth diocese did he deliver a charge which was anything like as long as the published charges of Glyn Simon when he was Bishop of Llandaff. It was characteristic of Green that he used his first Visitation charge to emphasise the part that the clergy should play in Church teaching as the "paramount need of our congregations at the present moment". He stressed the value of the Church Catechism in helping the parish priest to instruct his congregation before they formed opinions of their own "without the benefit of his help" which the parish priest would later denounce, although his people had only drifted into false views "because he has failed in his duty". At his second Visitation charge, Green urged the parochial clergy to accept the expertise of the missioners who would be conducting the Church Crusade throughout the industrial areas of the diocese in June 1928.

The years of Green's episcopate were not easy for the industrial areas of the new diocese and between his two Visitation charges had come the general strike of May 1926. In fact the general strike had cut short a holiday that Green and his wife were spending at Ventnor in the Isle of Wight. They arrived home on the evening before the strike began on Tuesday 4th May. Green noted the strike in his diary but otherwise he declined to make any comment upon it. He believed that his best contribution to the welfare of the industrial areas had been made when he provided them with the church-buildings that they had needed for half a century, and he would remember 1926 as the year in which he had consecrated St. Luke's parish church at Abercarn.

Many will feel that in the controversial matter of a cathedral for the new diocese, Green had much sense on his side. Many others have privately thanked God that the proposal for a separate cathedral establishment at Newport was never carried out. The resources that such an establishment would have drained from a small diocese in a town where churches already proliferated would have been burdensome. In the matter of the reorganisation of the rural deaneries to fit them for a more effective role, Green was thinking of possibilities for the future that have still not been realised, although it might be argued that Green's aim in planning a more vigorous rural deanery association was not dissimilar from that of the creators of rectorial benefices and those who urge a greater partnership in Ministry within the rural deanery to-day. Green never lacked the courage to reorganise in the interests of renewal.

6. Bishop of Bangor

At the time of disestablishment in 1920, the four diocesan Bishops of the Church in Wales were old men. John Owen of St. David's was the only Welsh bishop then under seventy years of age. The youngest died first and on Bishop Owen's death in 1926, his diocese passed to his archdeacon, David Lewis Prosser, a contemporary of Frank Morgan at Keble College. Bishop Edwards, aged seventy-one in 1920, continued as Archbishop until he was constrained to resign in 1934. Joshua Pritchard Hughes, son of a bishop whose only distinction was to have been the first Welsh-speaking Welshman to be appointed to a Welsh see since 1715, continued as Bishop of Llandaff until 1931. Watkin Herbert Williams of Bangor, the oldest of the four, failed to prevent the separation of Wales from Canterbury, and retired in 1925 at the age of eighty. His successor Dr. Daniel Davies, was the first bishop elected to an ancient see by the electoral college of the Church in Wales.

Three years later the untimely death of Dr. Davies provided the electoral college with its first opportunity to translate a bishop within the new province, and Charles Green was elected Bishop of Bangor at the age of sixty-four. The translation or transference of a bishop from one diocese to another was forbidden by the Council of Nicea in 325. This prohibition had never been strictly obeyed and many favoured translation as a way of providing more onerous dioceses with experienced bishops. All too often the remuneration of the richer see became more important than the responsibilities, and the translation of bishops could hardly be judged a historical success particularly in Wales where the dioceses had been only poor stepping-stones to English dioceses. Wales had suffered so much from this policy until the second half of the nineteenth century that it is a little surprising to see translation so readily revived in the new province.

The electoral college of the Church in Wales met in Bangor Cathedral on Tuesday 25th September, 1928 and elected Charles Green Bishop of Bangor. His election was confirmed by the Synod of Bishops of the Church in Wales on 17th October, 1928 by which act, as he noted, he "became actually Bishop of Bangor at 12.30 p.m." It was the eve of the seventh birthday of the diocese of Monmouth which became *sede vacante* until Green's friend Gilbert Joyce became Monmouth's second bishop in November.

The synodical act of translating Green to Bangor was effected by a letter from the Synod of bishops to the Archbishop of Wales informing him of the confirmation of Green's election by themselves. Since the Synod was composed of Archbishop Edwards and the three other bishops apart from Green, the synodical act of translating a bishop might be described as a letter addressed to himself by the chief signatory of that letter. Even funnier is the fact that Green, the subject of the letter, almost certainly compiled it himself and he published it nine years later in an appendix to his *Setting of the Constitution* as a model for the future.

Green was enthroned at Bangor Cathedral on Tuesday 30th October, 1928. Some may well wonder why he chose to go north to Bangor at the age of sixty-four. His age need not worry us since his health was good, although his wife suffered from asthma that did not improve during her stay in Bangor and after Green's death, the Hon. Mrs. Green returned south to her sister in Brecon. The short answer, and the only proper one for Green, was that he had been called by the Holy Spirit through his election by the Church in Wales. It is possible to be cynical about any method of appointing bishops and to see the attendant danger of lobbying in an electoral-college system. Green would probably have become a bishop under any system. He was almost certainly canvassed beforehand about his willingness to go to Bangor. He had certainly received at least one letter from a senior academic in Bangor who wanted Green to become bishop there to strengthen the link between the academic and ecclesiastical life of the cathedral city. In the whole diocese of Monmouth there was no institution of higher education and the presence of a university college on his door-step must have been an attraction to Green. After his election the principal of University College, Bangor looked forward to a "continuance of the close co-operation between religious and educational movements in north Wales that has been a pleasant feature of recent years".

In view of the age of Archbishop Edwards and the death of his able lieutenant Bishop Owen, the Church in Wales saw Green as Owen's successor in that role and an obvious successor to the Archbishop. It was convenient to have Green in the neighbouring diocese to Edwards.

To a man of Green's temperament it was no mean thing to be bishop of such an ancient diocese. In contrast with the new diocese of Monmouth, Bangor had its own well-established cathedral and diocesan organisations. The cathedral had been restored and cared for by a succession of able deans after 1868, two of them Green's predecessors as Vicar of Aberdare, Evan Lewis and Henry Thomas Edwards. Lewis had preceded Edwards at Aberdare and succeeded him at Bangor. Lewis was a pioneer of the Oxford Movement in Wales and both he and Edwards were associated with the intensive literary activity in Welsh at the end of the nineteenth century and the assertion of the proper place of the Welsh language in the life of the Church in Wales. The policy of appointing only Welsh-speaking bishops to Welsh dioceses after 1870 is attributed to a letter written by Henry Thomas Edwards, brother of the future Archbishop, to Gladstone in 1869.

In some respects Green's translation to Bangor seemed like a natural progression. His own father had spent the last twenty-five years of his ministry in north Wales and two distinguished Vicars of Aberdare had already trodden the path to the deanery at Bangor. Furthermore, old Griffith Roberts, the dean whom Green inherited, was already known to Green as a former Rector of Dowlais and Canon Missioner in Llandaff. Roberts belonged to the generation before Green as did the Archdeacon of Merioneth, John Lloyd-Jones, but the Archdeacon of Bangor, Albert Owen Evans was Green's own age. By 1928 Archdeacon Evans had proved himself a man of sound learning with no less than four scholarly works to his credit since 1918. Thoroughly Welsh in sympathy, Evans had an unrivalled knowledge of the Welsh Bible and Book of Common Prayer and a library that rivalled that of Green himself.

In terms of acres or square miles the Diocese of Bangor was more than twice the size of Monmouth and was therefore more demanding upon the Bishop. The population of the diocese was however less than half of Monmouth and had actually declined since 1925. Once co-extensive with the ancient principality of Gwynedd, the diocese in 1928 comprised the island of Anglesey, most of the county of Caernarfon and parts of the counties of Montgomery and Merioneth.

Green was no stranger to the diocese as he revealed to the Diocesan Conference of 3rd October, 1929, his first since becoming Bishop. In his early days at Oxford he had spent a holiday with his maternal uncle, the rector of Dolbenmaen and Penmorfa and he had read the lessons for the first time in Welsh in the ancient church at Penmorfa. The Conference was amused to learn that Green had once applied unsuccessfully for the vacant curacy at Llanllechid where Evan Lewis had worked before becoming Vicar of Aberdare. Green had admired Archdeacon John Evans who was then Rector of Llanllechid, but Aberdare had really been a better training-ground for a future Archbishop.

After Green's enthronement at Bangor, he and his wife and their four servants had to remain in their house at Newport because Bishopscourt in Bangor was not ready for occupation. Bishop Daniel Davies had lived there for three years after Glyngarth Palace at Menai Bridge had been abandoned by the diocese, but much work was carried out at Bishopscourt before the Green household moved there in April 1929.

In the meantime the furniture of the Bishop's chapel at Jesmond was transferred to King's Hill in November 1928 in time for the election of Archdeacon Joyce as Bishop of Monmouth. The work of the Diocese of Bangor had to continue and Green spent the winter months on the Confirmations that his predecessor had arranged and in other engagements in Bangor. He travelled hundreds of miles by road and rail, staying at hotels and vicarages *en route* to reach his destination on time. During these months his diaries sound more than usually like the peregrinations of a medieval bishop's itinerary.

With the help of Joseph Morgan, Rector of Panteg (Monmouth) and a former curate at Aberdare, Green travelled by car to Aberdovey on Monday 19th November, 1928. After spending the night there, they continued next day to Machynlleth and then Towyn for Confirmations. On Wednesday they drove north to Dolgellau and south-east to Llanidloes on Thursday. Friday was spent on Confirmations further north at Criccieth and Maentwrog and Saturday at Caernarfon. Sunday was the turn of the parishes of Penmaenmawr and Llandudno and on Monday Green was confirming at Conway. Few bishops would have envied Green such a week in north Wales at the end of November. He then travelled to St. Asaph where he spent a few days with Archbishop Edwards before returning to Newport on Saturday 1st December.

As Vicar of Aberdare, Green had attached great importance to the careful preparation of candidates for Confirmation. As a bishop he was equally careful with the addresses that he delivered to the newly-confirmed, and he expected the Confirmation services to be arranged and conducted with equal care. We do not know what he thought of the arrangements that had been made for his first Confirmations at Bangor. We do know that a week later he was preparing his "Directions for Confirmation" for his printers at Bangor and these directions greatly assisted the parish priests in the arrangement and ordering of the services.

March 1929 was almost entirely occupied with Confirmations. Knowlton, who had been Green's chauffeur at Newport, drove him from parish to parish and Cenydd Morgan, his domestic chaplain at Newport, accompanied him. They travelled from Aberdovey to Llanidloes; from Barmouth to Shrewsbury for a meeting of the Welsh Bishops; from Shrewsbury to Bettws-y-coed, thence to Beaumaris and so to Bangor Cathedral on 16th March. Cenydd Morgan then had to return to Newport, but Green continued on his way to Llangefni, south to Pwllheli and then north again to Amlwch. On 23rd March he was again at Bangor for another Confirmation, and he returned by car to Newport, after four more Confirmations, on Maundy Thursday. Small wonder that he spent the whole of Good Friday and most of Holy Saturday in bed at the order of his doctor.

Green moved into Bishopscourt on 25th April, 1929. On the following Monday, R. Cybi Jones, one of the minor canons became his private secretary. Only a brave man with a very orderly mind would have enjoyed such a position, and one of Jones's successors who later became Archdeacon of Merioneth, has described how all Green's correspondence "which was not personal was typed and copies kept in a filing system which was as efficient as human infirmity could make it". Before Archdeacon Wallis Thomas could become Green's private secretary in October 1937 he had to receive instruction in the use of the Dictaphone and take lessons in typewriting in Bangor for which Green agreed to pay "provided you complete them before Minor Canon Evans gives his duties over to you"! There was also a strict code by which Green subscribed his name to his letters. A humble parish priest got "Yours very truly"; a Cathedral canon received the accolade of "Yours sincerely", which became "Yours very sincerely" when he became further air-borne.

Green spent the end of April and most of May 1929 settling into Bishopscourt. On Thursday 30th May, he and his wife went by train to Newport to vote in the general election. Next day they were disappointed to learn that Newport had returned a Labour M.P. for the first and only time in Green's lifetime. They had received the news at Paddington where they had spent the night on their way to Windsor. They visited their sister and brother-in-law, Margaret and Parry de Winton at Eton. Margaret was Lord Merthyr's youngest child and she had been close to her oldest sister, Katharine Green, since the death of her mother in 1902. Green and his wife were fond of their de Winton nephews and it was with Margaret de Winton that Mrs. Green went to live after Green's death.

After a week at Windsor, Green travelled to Oxford where he stayed with Dr. Francis Pember, the Warden of All Souls and Vice Chancellor. He preached to the University at St. Mary's as select preacher on Sunday 9th June, and returned to London on the next day to attend the meetings of Bishops at Lambeth under the presidency of the new Archbishop, Lang. In churchmanship and social outlook Green had much in common with Lang, but in one matter Lang gladly acknowledged Green's superiority. That was the care and attention that Green paid to the preparation of his sermons and public addresses. "It puts me to shame" wrote Lang to Green on the eve of the Silver Jubilee of King George V, "when I compare the care and thoroughness of your sermon and the reading that lies behind it with my hasty and haphazard way of composing my own sermons and addresses".

Green returned to Bangor on 14th June to continue his work in the diocese. He had to prepare for the Ordination on 29th June, St. Peter's Day and he was particularly concerned that the Ordination service, always longer than most other services, should not be unduly long. That particular service lasted for two hours, but his next Ordination on Saturday 21st September, St. Matthew's Day, was completed in an hour and a half. At this stage in his episcopate he held Ordinations four times a year on red-letter saints' days, but during the next decade the pattern of one Ordination in Welsh and one in English every year seemed to become established in the diocese.

Between the two Ordinations, Green had to spend a week in bed in July through a painful stone in the kidney. This did not prevent him from keeping up with his reading and writing and he had fully recovered by the end of July when he was preparing Lady Caroline Paget, a daughter of the Marquess of Anglesey, for her Confirmation. In September Green and his wife spent a fortnight at the Moorland Hotel in Haytor Rocks in Devon, which was their favourite holiday-spot in the years between the wars.

Green returned from holiday in time for the September Ordination. He faced his first Diocesan Conference at Bangor on 3rd October, 1929 and showed that he was fully in command of his diocese and conscious of its needs and opportunities. His first year in Bangor had been busy but Green was never in a rush and he would not face any task without preparation. Upon his sudden translation to Bangor he had been forced to cancel his retreat, arranged for November 1928, at the house of the Society of St. John the Evangelist at Oxford. This retreat in November had been an annual event in Green's calendar since he became a bishop and he continued it until the pressures upon him made the annual retreat impossible and he had to be content with a brief annual visit to St. Edward's house in Westminster to make his confession. In November 1929 Green was able to attend the retreat at Oxford for four days, and he returned to Bangor refreshed for diocesan duties at the end of that month. In December he wrote the article that he had been invited to contribute to the volume, *Episcopacy Ancient and Modern*, edited by Claude Jenkins and K.D. Mackenzie (S.P.C.K. 1930). In that volume of essays there is an article that Green might well have written. It tells forthrightly and honestly of the increase in the power of the bishops in the disestablished Church in Wales and it emphasises the extent to which Cyprian's ideal of episcopacy has been achieved. That article was written by Chancellor Hopkin-James, Vicar of St. Martin's Roath, perhaps wisely since Green could hardly have been objective about the development of episcopal power in Wales. Green contributed the essay on episcopacy in the Roman Catholic Church and he demonstrated how clearly he understood the theology and practice of episcopacy within the Roman Communion at that time without losing sight of what was, for him, of paramount importance: "The problem whether the whole arrangement between Pope and bishop is consistent with the Divine institution of Episcopacy, which is an article of faith for Roman Catholics, or with the actual course of ecclesiastical history, lies outside the scope of this essay, which has been to describe as accurately as possible, Episcopacy as it is to-day in the Roman Catholic Church".

It does seem strange to-day that Professor Claude Jenkins should have invited a Welsh Anglican Bishop to pontificate upon the pope, but Green greatly desired reunion with the Roman Catholic Church. When he was Bishop of Monmouth he had personally received from the author, Viscount Halifax, two printed addresses on the subject of reunion with Rome and he had these privately bound for himself together with other papers on reunion with Rome including the report on the Malines Conversations 1921-25. These conversations at Malines had been initiated by Halifax and were held under the presidency of Cardinal Mercier, Archbishop of Malines, whose death in January 1926 brought the conversations to an end. The Anglican participants included Green's friend and mentor, B.J. Kidd of Keble. To Kidd Archbishop Davidson expressed his fear that the publication of a record of the conversations might look like "truckling to the Roman See".So it seemed to those for whom Hensley Henson acted as the highest episcopal spokesman, but Green would happily have aligned himself with those who like,

"Armitage, Armitage, Robinson Gore,
Halifax, Frere and Kidd
are constantly seen on the way to Malines
and no longer try to be hid."

The attempts at Christian reunion in the 1920s. originated with the Appeal to all Christian people at the Lambeth Conference of 1920. Apart from the enormous fund of good-will created by the Appeal, there was little progress to report to the Lambeth Conference of 1930 except for the limited achievement of Malines and the acceptance by the Orthodox and Old Catholic Churches of the validity of Anglican Orders.

The Lambeth Conference of 1930 facilitated the progress towards full communion between the Anglican and Old Catholic Churches and welcomed the progress towards reunion in the Church of South India, but it was not a great conference and the press, and Hensley Henson, believed that the only significant decision of the conference was the approval that it gave to contraceptives. "Mainly" wrote Henson, "the business of the Conference has been in the hands of the English Bishops ... and the bishops from Wales have hardly uttered a word".[12]

The Welsh bishops clearly had the sense to realise that the mediocrity of the conference would be attributed to the leadership of the English bishops, and having nothing to contribute on the subject of contraception, they wisely remained silent or in Green's case simply stayed away. He was in Bangor on diocesan business while the discussions of the conference committees were taking place in the second half of July, but he returned to Lambeth for the committee reports on 28th July and he stayed there until 7th August when he travelled to Llanelli for the National Eisteddfod meetings at which he presided on 8th August.

Green returned to London for the concluding service of the Lambeth Conference on Sunday 10th August. His own contribution to the conference had been severely limited by the pressure of events and by personal bereavement. At the personal level Green could not attend the Quiet Day for the Bishops at Fulham, to which he had looked forward, nor the first day's session of the conference on 7th July, because of the death of his brother-in-law, Richard Morten, the husband of his youngest sister, Edith. Earlier in the year his brother Sebert, a doctor of medicine who had retired after a very distinguished career in the Army, died on 5th February and was buried at Albrighton where Green's brother Kenneth was Vicar. On his return from Sebert's funeral, Green had to prepare for his impending primary visitation charge at Bangor Cathedral.

Green spent many hours on the sessions of his first General Visitation of the diocese during the spring and early summer. In addition to this there were the usual Confirmations; Ordinations in the Cathedral in March, June, September and December and meetings of the bishops at Lambeth to prepare for the Conference at the beginning of June. At the end of June he had to join in the celebrations for the bi-centenary of the beginning of the work of Griffith Jones of Llanddowror in founding the Welsh circulating schools.

On the evening of Saturday 21st June, 1930, Green preached an erudite sermon in Welsh in Bangor Cathedral in commemoration of the work of Griffith Jones through the Circulating Schools. Green chose as his text the words of Hebrews chapter 13, verse 7: "Remember your leaders, those who spoke to you the word of God; consider the outcome of their life, and imitate their faith". Green recognised the achievement of the Circulating Schools in raising the level of literacy in Wales during the fifty years after 1730. The motive of Griffith Jones in seeking to save men's souls by enlightening their minds was also fully approved by Green not least because all education for Green, as for Griffith Jones, was religious education.

There is no evidence to suggest that Green ever experienced the kind of religious conversion that Griffith Jones knew and inspired in others. Nor did Green approve of the way in which the Methodist revival developed in Wales under the leadership of some who had been associated with Griffith Jones. At the same time, Green was proud to be Welsh and proud to be a descendant, through the redoubtable Ebenezer Morris of Llanelli, of the Methodist Biblical commentator Peter Williams.

Charles Green was always sympathetic to Welsh national consciousness and aspirations. He firmly supported the developments in Welsh cultural life that culminated in the foundation of the three great national institutions, the University, the Library and the Museum. He became a member of the Court of Governors of University College Cardiff in 1914. In 1933 he became a member of the Council and Court of Governors of University College Bangor. He served on the Council of the National Museum of Wales from 1935 and of the National Library from 1936. He was also a Vice-President of the Honourable Society of Cymmrodorion. In August 1930 he had been admitted to the Gorsedd as a "Derwydd" and in 1931 he had the pleasure of welcoming the National Eisteddfod to Bangor.

What a welcome! Characteristically Green welcomed the Eisteddfod with High Mass in Bangor Cathedral. The Eisteddfod had actually opened on Bank Holiday Monday, 3rd August. Green attended the opening, but spent the afternoon preparing for his service on Wednesday. On Tuesday he attended the Gorsedd at 8 a.m. and sang the Gorsedd prayer. He presided at the morning session, attended the crowning of the Bard in the early afternoon and later presided at the meeting of the Council for preserving rural Wales. Wednesday was Green's great day when Bangor Cathedral was filled for the High Mass to welcome the Eisteddfod to Bangor. The behaviour was "devout and reverent and the solemn silence after the Consecration was very impressive". There was no sermon, but the eighty-six year old dean, Griffith Roberts, read a list of biddings. Those who wished to make their communions had sent in their names beforehand so that the number of communicants was not large. It was noted that many prominent members of the Gorsedd were seen in the processions of clergy and in the congregation. The *Church Times* on the following Friday reported that incense was not used, but described Green's High Mass as "a gesture of sympathy with Welsh national aspirations".

Canon Frederic Hood wrote that Green had firm convictions but he was always eirenic towards those who disagreed with him. Through kindness with firmness Green was able to lead people far without antagonising them. The Eisteddfod week in Bangor passed off happily without bitterness and without compromise but having achieved much in mutual understanding.

Some of Green's actions in 1931 were to be of later significance for his home diocese of Llandaff. At the beginning of that year Green knew that the Bishop of Llandaff would be retiring on 24th February. Within a month of that date, the Archbishop as President of the Electoral College, would issue the summons to elect his successor. Who would succeed the eighty-four year old bishop?

In January Green wrote to Father Timothy Rees of Mirfield a letter that he clearly regarded as important since he recorded its postage, but we can only guess at its contents since neither the letter nor its reply have been preserved. Green had known Timothy Rees well since they had worked together at Aberdare: Timothy Rees had been a student and later chaplain of St. Michael's College while Green was the Vicar. It seems certain that Timothy Rees was Green's candidate for the diocese of Llandaff and he could not have picked a better one at that time. The Electoral College did not take long to elect Timothy Rees Bishop of Llandaff on Thursday 26th March at Llandaff Cathedral, although the biography of Timothy Rees incorrectly gives the date of his election as 25th March. The Archbishop was unwell and Green celebrated the Eucharist instead of him, but Green's excitement at the forthcoming election caused him to forget to say Matins!

In that same year Green appointed John Morgan, Timothy Rees's successor at Llandaff and a future Archbishop of Wales, to the vacant prebend of Llanfair in Bangor Cathedral. At the same time, Glyn Simon, destined to succeed John Morgan as Bishop of Llandaff in 1957, had just started his work as Warden of Church Hostel in Bangor and one of Green's examining chaplains. Church Hostel, a hall of residence for Anglican students at Bangor, had a clerical warden but lacked a chapel. Green thought that Church Hostel should have its own chapel and he not only launched the appeal fund to pay for it but, characteristically he made a very generous personal donation towards the total cost of £1,600. Green announced this appeal to his Diocesan Conference in September 1932. Fourteen months later on 7th November, 1933 the chapel of Church Hostel was opened and Green celebrated the first Eucharist there.

To that same Diocesan Conference in September 1932 Green announced the celebration of the centenary of the Oxford Movement in the following year culminating in a solemn Eucharist in the open air at Keble College on 14th July. On that day one hundred years earlier John Keble had preached his Assize Sermon in the University Church, St. Mary's, at Oxford before his Majesty's Judges of Assize, and Newman later considered that day to have been the start of the movement.

The impact of the Oxford Movement was summarised by another Keble Bishop, A.F. Winnington-Ingram of London, preaching in Hendon Parish Church in 1930 as "bringing back to our Church order and discipline and rightful ceremonial, and the constant use of the sacraments. We have only to compare the Church of England to-day with that of a hundred years ago to see how much we owe to the Oxford Movement".[13] Green was concerned that the disestablished Church in Wales should understand the message of the Oxford Movement.

To this end Green prepared with characteristic thoroughness a special sermon that he preached with only slight variations in four centres throughout Wales; at St. David's College, Lampeter; in Llandaff Cathedral; in Bangor Cathedral and in Machynlleth Parish Church. The sermon was first preached at St. David's College at a Sung Eucharist to celebrate the Oxford Movement centenary on Saturday 6th May and it was published by Green in July "at the request of some who heard it".

In some respects Green's sermon followed the line of Keble's original Assize sermon but in others it was very different from Keble's sermon which was preached from the text in 1 Samuel 12:23, "As for me, God forbid that I should sin against the Lord in ceasing to pray for you". The apostasy of the Israelites at the time of Samuel in demanding to have a king like the other nations, was not irredeemable since their repentance would bring deliverance from God. Keble sought to identify such apostasy in the State-Church relationship of his day. What mattered to Keble was the principle of parliamentary interference in the affairs of the Church which was a divinely-created society.

With that principle Green wholeheartedly agreed. His own text was taken from verses four, five and six of chapter four of the first letter of St. John in the Revised Version, a translation that he always preferred to the Authorised. The Johannine distinction between the world organised apart from God and those who belong to God afforded ample opportunity to emphasise the existence of the Church as the Divine Society "sufficient by Divine Grace to teach and to act in freedom from the world". "Back to the Church" he proclaimed "was the call from Oxford in 1833; and as we shall see, it was needed".

Green then departed greatly from the pattern of Keble's sermon by proceeding to deliver a lengthy exposition of the course of Church history since the Reformation, during which he emphasised what he understood to be the autonomy of the Church through the activities of Convocation from 1533 until 1717. This central part of the sermon he later published as an appendix to the *Setting of the Constitution.*

Green's interpretation of the Acts of the Reformation Settlement was entirely in line with the belief of the Tractarians that what mattered was what actually happened through the Reformation Statutes and not what people thought had happened. "The teaching and practices of the Continental Reformers do not concern us. The Church of England deliberately did not follow them". Green followed Hooker in condemning those who looked only to John Calvin as an authority so that "the formularies of the Church of England came to be laden with glosses and interpretations of which the plain grammatical language was innocent". According to Green, the Oxford Movement cleared away "the mass of super-imposed ideas and commentaries from the formularies of the Church".

An objective modern historian would probably say that not all the disciples of the Oxford Movement were as certain about the pure and Catholic motives of the English Reformers as Green. The English Reformation was not purely English: the English Reformers were greatly influenced by their European precursors. Luther had been excommunicated before Cranmer was ordained.

Green also tended to take the preambles to the Reformation statutes, always replete with Tudor propaganda, at their face value and, in the notable case of the Act in Restraint of Appeals to Rome, to twist the original purpose from a justification of the independence of England from Rome because "this realm of England is an empire" to a royal assertion of the guaranteed independence of the government of the Church through Convocation. Both Henry VIII and Elizabeth did indeed allow Convocation to function provided that it did not operate against their wills, and Elizabeth used Convocation in the exercise of her Royal Prerogative against Parliament's attempts to interfere with her Religious Settlement.

Ironically, apart from its temporary demise under Oliver Cromwell, the crisis for Convocation came when Hoadly, Bishop of Bangor, was threatened with Synodical condemnation because of a sermon that he preached before George I in 1717 in which he claimed that no visible Church authority was justified in the light of the Gospels. The protest of the lower house of Convocation caused the king to prorogue Convocation which was not allowed to meet again for the transaction of business until 1852. "This new, and high-handed policy of the state", said Green "proved disastrous to religion in our land" so that "by 1833 the position of the Church was parlous in the extreme. The spirit of an Erastian utilitarianism was rampant in political and journalistic circles". Green's words here adequately explain the climate of opinion when Keble preached his Assize sermon, but Green was really hoist with his own petard, since the same Reformation Parliament that approved the Act in Restraint of Appeals had also embodied in its legislation the Submission of the Clergy under which the Crown later deprived Convocation of the right to discuss business, and many historians would argue that the spirit of an Erastian utilitarianism was facilitated by nothing more than by the Reformation Parliament.

At the end of his sermon Green referred to the "bewilderment into which the Act of Disestablishment threw churchfolk in Wales". "Only those" he concluded, "who had learnt the lessons of the Oxford Movement, who had faith in the Church as a divine society...could help the Church in Wales to recover its poise, and bravely take up its appointed task". No-one did more than Charles Green to help the Church in Wales to do these things, but there is a fundamental contradiction in what he implies since "the spirit of an Erastian utilitarianism" had not only brought about the disestablishment of the Church in Wales, as it had produced Keble's sermon, but provided one of the best reasons for preferring the disestablishment of the Church.

Professor Owen Chadwick has written that Keble's Assize sermon was more representative of an old-fashioned high churchmanship that claimed "to retain the rightful privileges of the Establishment" rather than to assert "the independent and divine status of the Church, whether the Church was established or disestablished".[14] Green had opposed disestablishment and his opposition seemed more to reflect the high churchmanship of Keble's sermon that liked the privileges of establishment, though Green's tractarianism did not separate this claim to rightful privileges from the emphasis upon the

Church's divinely-commissioned nature in the face of those who regarded it as little more than an inconvenient human organisation that impeded their national aspirations. He lived long enough to recognise that disestablishment had brought great benefits to Wales, but it is not untrue to say that Green never really faced up to the implications of disestablishment for the Church in Wales. In a disestablished Church he still wanted "to retain the rightful privileges of the Establishment" and there was much in Green's mental outlook which came dangerously close to Erastianism although he was careful to retain the distinction between Caesar's jurisdiction and that of God. What is surprising is the trust that Green, and others like him, reposed in the Establishment so soon after the failure of the Prayer Book measures of 1928.

Green returned to the newly-consecrated chapel of Church Hostel Bangor on 19th December, 1933 to conduct a retreat for those who were to be ordained in Bangor Cathedral on St. Thomas's Day, two days later. Green's addresses to the ordinands, as one would expect, were carefully prepared. They were also clearly expressed, but above all, they were practical and simple as they applied to the lives that the newly-ordained clergymen would be leading.

Green's addresses to his ordinands were prepared under seven headings: the inward motive for ordination; the Call, mediated through the Church, since all clergymen, in whatever order of ministry, are men under authority; the study of Scripture; Diligence in Prayers; Public Ministrations; Pastoral Care and personal and family life.

Personal discipline, said Green, is essential for all Christians, but especially in the life of a clergyman. It was essential that men whose ministries were to be effective should be men who regularly studied the Scriptures and whose spiritual growth was developed through prayer. Of the study of Scripture, Green said, "No clergyman has ever found this obligation easy to fulfil. Yet there is no clergyman whose ministry has been worth anything but he has tried his best to overcome the interruptions, distractions and difficulties which beset the parish priest". This was sensible practical advice, revealing both astuteness and humility in one to whom regular study of the Scriptures seemed to come easily. "You must have a time-table" he said. "Get up early in the morning". "Learning Scripture by heart is most beneficial".

When it came to Prayer, Green stressed that obligation of every clergyman to say Morning and Evening Prayer daily; to pray for others and to practise mental prayer for which he would need instruction. In his sermons the priest should cover the whole ground of Christian doctrine by mapping out courses of instruction in his study. In his reverent administration of the sacraments he should "gradually restore the Eucharist to its rightful place among the services of the Church". In their pastoral care all clergymen should cultivate the habit of regular pastoral visiting while they were still deacons. It was ordinary enough advice, but Green knew that it could have extraordinary effects if it were followed.

Green's candidates for Ordination received only sound, practical advice. There was no academic content in these addresses nor did he set his candidates an examination before they were made deacons because he accepted the general ordination examination as sufficient proof that his deacons were "apt and meet for their learning". In fact most of those who listened to his addresses at their ordination retreats were already University graduates who had also spent time at a theological college. As far as possible, Green insisted upon such a course of study. In 1935 he could proudly claim that "of the 57 men ordained by me, or for me, since my translation to Bangor in 1928, 51 were graduates". He also expected his ordinands to be proficient in Welsh and he thought that clergymen should be well-educated and trained to be able to minister effectively in a world where graduates were "being poured out of our provincial universities in a constant stream" and every secular profession was "insisting upon a prolonged and expert training for its members". Green thought that the parish priest should study ecclesiastical law at least as far as it related to the parish under the Constitution of the Church in Wales. This would enable him to be a more efficient administrator. But Green knew that a parish priest had to be more than an administrator and even more than a preacher. "A man with a crooked vision of life, or an uncontrolled temper, or an untempered pride, is manifestly not suitable for the cure of souls" he declared.

Green clearly expected high standards from his parish priests, but they were no higher than he demanded from himself, and many tributes have been paid to the pastoral care that he gave to his pastors and to his "solicitude, his anxious readiness to help in any difficulty, personal or parochial". Such was the tribute paid to him in the *Western Mail* by his successor at Aberdare on the morning after Green had been elected Archbishop of Wales in November 1934.

As well as clerical education and training, Green continued to be keenly interested in the instruction and training of lay people after his translation to Bangor.

Green had bemoaned the untimely death of his predecessor and praised the latter's contribution to Church schools at his first Diocesan Conference at Bangor. Dr. Daniel Davies had raised large sums of money for Church schools in the diocese and Green identified himself with his predecessor's policy. Green was forward-looking about the proposals of the Hadow Report of 1926 for the termination of all primary education at the age of eleven and the creation of Central Schools for secondary education until the age of fifteen. Green urged

Churchpeople not to oppose the Central Schools where he hoped that denominational instruction would be secured. At the same time he believed that Church elementary schools would still have their work to do in instructing children in "our most holy faith".

As it turned out, the Hadow Report was not implemented in Green's lifetime, but his concern for the provision of instruction in the faith remained strong. He believed that all Churchpeople needed to be "better grounded in our faith" in order "deliberately to witness for Christ" before the "scoffing and vindictive world". Such was his concern in 1929, but he had deepened and clarified this by 1932 into a call for Churchpeople to understand how their faith differed from that of Nonconformity. He told his Diocesan Conference that the Church in Wales "claimed to be the true and original representative of the Holy Catholic Church in this land" but he was deeply concerned because, "ever since 1914...there had been a cessation of the regular instruction in Church History which prevailed before 1914". The Church Defence campaign had produced Churchpeople who knew what they believed. Now that the Church in Wales was more closely identified with national aspirations and was making converts among the Free Churches, there was a greater need than ever for careful preparations of such candidates for Confirmation, and Green requested his parish priests to give extra time and attention to them. "It is difficult" he said, "for those who have been nurtured elsewhere to grasp the true position and assimilate the spirit of the Church in Wales". Green commended for study a book that had been published in Bangor in 1896 and was still on sale there. The book, *Y Grefydd Catholig* (The Catholic Religion) was in fact a translation by Benjamin Thomas from the original English version of Vernon Staley.

Green was uncompromising about the need to insist upon the Catholic heritage of the Church in Wales and to refute the sentimentality that suggested that there was no difference between the Church in Wales and the other religious bodies. If Churchpeople "found no difference in faith and practice between themselves and the divers denominations which were around them, then the sooner they dissolved their ecclesiastical polity and disappeared from the field, the better for themselves, and the better for Wales".

Modern supporters of the ecumenical movement will rightly say that Green would have done better to concentrate upon those beliefs that the Church in Wales shared with the Free Churches and less upon their differences, but the contemporary scene seemed otherwise to Green and he never changed his mind. He could not compromise what he believed to be the truth and he regarded as nothing more than sentimentality the belief that Free Churchmen and Church communicants could share communion at the Lord's Table when they were so deeply divided over such fundamental issues of Christian belief as the nature of the Ministry and the Sacraments.

When Green appointed a new Dean of Bangor Cathedral in 1941, he specified five conditions that had to be accepted by his nominee before his appointment. One of these stated clearly "that you will be firm in the teaching and practices of the Church, and not yield to the pressures of Nonconformity, nor allow undenominationalism to get a footing in the cathedral. Hitherto firmness has caused no difficulty; the public and Public Bodies attend in force on public occasions, but the clergy alone officiate".

We should not judge Green too harshly for this in view of the date and the fact that at least two of his successors in the see of Bangor continued to be firm on this matter and had cause to be grateful to him. Even now the progress of the ecumenical movement in Wales has hardly been so significant as to allow us with any justification to accuse Green of being antediluvian.

7. Archbishop of Wales

On 1st June, 1934 Alfred George Edwards had been Archbishop of Wales for fourteen years. He was in his eighty-sixth year and was the only bishop in Wales who had been appointed by the Crown. Like all old men of spirit, he could be cantankerous if anyone tried to organise him, particularly at his ordination services, and leading figures in the Church in Wales began to wonder how they could ever persuade him to retire.

Archbishop Edwards resigned from the diocese of St. Asaph and thereby from the Archbishopric on 25th July, St. James' Day, 1934. As senior diocesan bishop, Charles Green became the Guardian of the spiritualities of the vacant diocese of St. Asaph, which meant that he was responsible for instituting clergymen to benefices or collating them, where the right of presentation lay with the bishop; licensing curates; ordaining priests and deacons and carrying out the Confirmations that had been arranged. It was fortunate that St. Asaph already had a suffragan bishop, Thomas Lloyd, whom Green immediately appointed to act as his commissary while the diocese was vacant.

Until the election of a new bishop of St. Asaph, there could be no Archbishop of Wales. Green had to wait until 23rd October, 1934, when Bishop Havard had been enthroned at St. Asaph, before he could summon the Archbishop's Electoral College to meet at Llandrindod on Thursday 8th November.

In the meantime Green had acted as archbishop in all but name since 25th July. He had presided over the meetings of the Governing Body at Llandrindod in September where he had delivered a valediction to Archbishop Edwards praising his contribution to the modern Church in Wales through his leadership of Church Defence. The claims of the Church in Wales had been strengthened by the tradition of Welsh-born and Welsh-speaking bishops to which Edwards belonged. As an educationist, Edwards had been determined that the Church should take her proper place in the educational systems of Wales. This much Green shared with Edwards. It is appropriate that Green had spent some time in April 1934 compiling a form of service in Welsh for the consecrating of a church, and he played a full part in the Jubilee celebrations of University College, Bangor which began in November.

On Thursday 8th November, Green celebrated the Eucharist at Holy Trinity Church, Llandrindod Wells at 8 a.m. He said Matins privately at 9.30 a.m. and was in the old parish church by 10.30 a.m. to preside over the Electoral College. In 1920 Archbishop Edwards had been elected by a unanimous vote of four bishops, including himself, but now, for the first time in the history of the Christian Church, elected lay representatives — three from each of the six dioceses — were present at the electoral college to vote with the eighteen clerical electors and the diocesan bishops.

Was it the novelty of the occasion and the inexperience of the electors on such an important occasion that enabled the *Western Mail* to publish so many details of this private meeting? At any rate the press reporters, avid for detail, did not have long to wait. By 11.30 a.m. the Bishop of Bangor had received 33 of the 41 votes and he became Archbishop-elect. Green was then proclaimed Archbishop and Metropolitan by the Bishops in Synod in the old parish church at 3 p.m. that same day and arrangements were set in hand for his enthronement as Archbishop at Bangor.

For the purpose of the enthronement, carried out by Bishop Prosser of St. David's, the Archbishop's throne, the gift of the late Mr. W.S. de Winton, had to be brought from St. Asaph to Bangor. This portable throne is a wooden replica of the stone throne of St. Augustine at Canterbury and it is always placed in the Archbishop's own cathedral.

Well before the enthronement Green had received scores of letters congratulating him upon his election as Archbishop. The letter from Dr. Kidd informed Green that he was the third Keble Archbishop, Perth, Capetown, Wales! Green was greatly honoured to become an honorary fellow of Keble in March 1935.

Official duties as Archbishop of Wales were now added to Green's already full list of engagements as Bishop of Bangor. On 29th November, 1934 Green and his wife attended the wedding of the Duke of Kent and Princess Marina at Westminster Abbey. On 11th May, 1935 Green was in Cardiff to join in the rapturous welcome for Edward, Prince of Wales when he visited the city with Lloyd George as part of the Silver Jubilee celebrations of the King. As Archbishop, Green had a seat at the main table at the luncheon in the City Hall.

The sermon that Green preached on the eve of the King's Silver Jubilee in May brought warm congratulations from Lambeth Palace, but the "thoroughness" to which Lang referred in his letter of acknowledgement, may well have been the key to Green's failing health as Archbishop. At seventy years of age other men, even in 1935, were relinquishing, not assuming, high office. At the same age Lloyd George himself was compiling his war memoirs in semi-retirement.

At the beginning of April 1935 Green had been kept in bed for a fortnight. He was upset because his Confirmations had been cancelled but some good came out of this illness because it forced him to admit that he could not do everything himself and so he commissioned a former Australian Bishop, W.F. Wentworth-Sheilds, the warden of St. Deiniol's Library, to act as his suffragan bishop from 10th April, 1935.

In his address to his Diocesan Conference on 22nd August, 1935 Green spoke of the practical difficulties of being Archbishop of Wales while living in Bangor. He was grateful for the help that he had received from the staff of the Representative Body at 39, Cathedral Road, but the truth was that Cardiff is a long way from Bangor and Green knew that he needed to be living in Cardiff for at least part of the year to deal with his duties as Metropolitan.

One of the Archbishop's duties which was not at Cardiff was of presiding over the Governing Body meetings which were then held at Llandrindod Wells. At his first meeting as Archbishop in September 1935, Green took the opportunity to remind the members of their close association with the Archbishop in the discipline of the province and to teach them that their authority had been given to them from above by the Synod of Bishops and not from below by other lay-people. They were all members of the Governing Body, said Green, "not through any secular honour ... but as persons consecrated by baptism, confirmation and communion to the service of their Lord".

Of the composition of the Governing Body at this time, the late Canon D. Parry-Jones, by no means a jaundiced observer, has written that "one looked in vain for the man with the blue veins in his hands and his face; absent also were the men in breeches and leggings whom one met in the marts and the fairs of the market towns of Wales". [15] Blue veins it may have lacked, but the Governing Body was not short of blue blood. The three hundred elected lay members whom Green bravely reminded that they were not members "through any secular honour" included at least six barons, ten baronets, five knights, eleven titled ladies, three sons of peers, two generals, one vice-admiral, one brigadier-general and sixteen colonels not to mention majors and captains. As they left Llandrindod in their Rolls-Royces "each with its liveried chauffeur" as Parry-Jones has so entertainingly described, one can only hope that they reflected on Green's speech. They did not have much else to reflect upon, because the only noteworthy business of that meeting was that the hours of marriage in the Church in Wales were lawfully extended from 3 p.m. to 6 p.m.. Certainly the members of the Governing Body at that time were not representative of the Welsh people nor even of Welsh Churchpeople although they had been elected through their diocesan conferences and they were probably the only people who had the leisure to spend a couple of days in the middle of the week at Llandrindod.

Outside Wales Green was becoming well-known as the ambassador of the Church in Wales. On 10th October, 1935 he addressed the Church Congress at Bournemouth which was eager to know what had been happening in Wales since disestablishment. Green's approach was positive and forward-looking. In 1935 there was little point in repeating the arguments of 1905. He ended his speech on an optimistic note: "You ask me, Is all well? I believe it is. True, our province is only fifteen years old. But the indications are good. Another will ask. Are you not in danger from isolation? I think not. There is free communication ... between England and Wales". From the perspective of fifteen years, that is probably how it looked to an archbishop who was half-English and had been educated in England. Fifty years later Green's denial of the danger of isolation would be less readily endorsed in the Church in Wales.

By October 1935 the upheaval of disestablishment was being overcome but the Church, like the nation, faced greater problems ahead without realising it. For the Church the problems of secularism and the crisis of faith were only just beginning. The National Government of Stanley Baldwin, returned in November 1935, had a large enough majority to carry through any domestic reform, but the legislation was negligible. One of the few reforms was the Matrimonial Causes Act, 1937, which began as a private member's bill to make divorce easier. Under the act no clergyman could be compelled to "solemnise the marriage of any person whose former marriage has been dissolved...and whose former husband or wife is still living", and the act itself was strongly opposed by the Church in Wales under Green's leadership.

It was almost a portent of the changing order that Mr. Frank Morgan died on 22nd December, 1935. Green, assisted by four bishops, officiated at his funeral service in Llandaff Cathedral on Christmas Eve. In his address to the next Governing Body in April 1936, Green paid eloquent tribute to Frank Morgan's keen mind and administrative ability. The Church in Wales was greatly indebted to Frank Morgan and Green knew better than most people how great was that debt.

The business of the Governing Body between 1936 and 1939 resembled the domestic legislation of the government. Intercommunion between the Church in Wales and the old Catholics was established in September 1937 and the use of proper psalms and "sundry prayers and thanksgivings" was authorised in 1938, but Green's addresses to the Governing Body were more concerned with "the disturbed condition of the world" (April 1936); "the mission of the Church in the world to-day" (September 1937) and "the critical international situation" (September 1938).

King George V died on 20th January 1936. Archbishop Green was at Westminster making his annual confession. On 11th December, Edward VIII abdicated and left the country the next morning as Duke of Windsor. George VI became king. Of the abdication crisis, Green wisely said nothing. The year of the three kings was a busy one for him since he was again involved in a general Visitation of his own diocese, two Ordination services at Bangor and the usual meetings of the Governing Body and the Diocesan Conference. His address to the conference at Portmadoc on 27th August was read for him by the Vicar, Canon David Jenkins, because Green had been suffering from shingles throughout August.

In his address, delivered by proxy, Green remarked upon the death of George V and the "apparent failure of the League of Nations". Most political commentators would probably have omitted the word "apparent" in view of the League's failure to intervene when Mussolini conquered Abyssinia and Hitler reoccupied the demilitarised zone of the Rhineland, but Green, like all men of good-will, had believed fervently in the League of Nations as a power for peace, and its demise was a bitter blow.

Most of Green's address was concerned with the publication by Sir Frederick Kenyon in February 1936 of "an almost complete copy of the Epistles of St. Paul at least a century older than the oldest of the authorities on which the text has hitherto rested". The order of the Pauline epistles in the manuscript that Kenyon had edited placed Hebrews immediately after Romans and Ephesians between 2 Corinthians and Galatians, perhaps suggesting that in Egypt both the letters to the Hebrews and Ephesians were considered to have been written by St. Paul. This particular manuscript was only one of a number that Kenyon edited after the discovery of the Chester Beatty Papyri in the sands of Egypt in 1930.

Was Green only burying his own head in the sands in thus dilating upon the importance of ancient papyri at such a time in the history of Europe? Perhaps he shared with Bishop Hensley Henson a desire "to make the most of every opportunity for widening the interests of the people by fastening attention on other matters than those which normally filled their minds". What Green actually did was to use Kenyon's publication as a springboard from which to deliver a further peroration on the importance of translations of the Scriptures and the work of the British and Foreign Bible Society. He went on, in true Tractarian spirit, to remind his audience that the faith proclaimed by the Scriptures is preached by the Church and that the "Rule of Faith is more ancient than the New Testament, and that the Church at first developed and grew without the New Testament. The Book was the product of the Church, not the Church the product of the Book".

Green quoted Harnack to assert that "the Christian religion before the days of Calvin was never the religion of a book in the same sense and degree as Islam", and he concluded with an appeal to Article 20 of the Thirty-nine Articles to remind his audience that the Church needed the Bible and the Bible needed the teaching of the Church.

Two years later, when celebrations were taking place to mark the seventh Jubilee of the Welsh Bible (1588) and the eighth Jubilee of the Great Bible in English (1538), Green took the opportunity of asking his Diocesan Conference: "What is the good of it all, if they remain unread, unpondered and disallowed?" Green believed that Christians should bear corporate testimony to Christ through their lives. When it came to Christian marriage, what was politically legal, namely the remarriage of divorced persons, was not necessarily ecclesiastically lawful. Here Green was harking back to 1937 and his condemnation of the Matrimonial Causes Act as "intended for the world and not for the Church".

At the Diocesan Conference at Caernarfon in 1937 Green had also returned to his anti-ecumenical stance and attacked the supporters of recent ecumenical conferences at Oxford (Life and Work) and at Edinburgh (Faith and Order). He had been influenced by reading W.K. Jordan's scholarly work, *The development of religious toleration in England*, and he used Jordan's three conceptions of the Church, the Catholic (universal) one; that of the sects and that of national Churches to claim that the final result of such ecumenical conferences as had taken place at Oxford and Edinburgh might be to show the irreducible nature of Jordan's three fundamental conceptions. If this proved to be so, Green thought that "their labour will not be in vain". If the term 'Church' meant different things to different people, then Green believed that it was idle to claim that one Church was the same as another. Terms should be defined because "in strict thought the God of John Wesley was not identical with the God of George Whitefield". Here Green returned to his fear and distrust of Calvinism particularly as he had seen it exhibited in Wales. Reference has already been made to Green's inability to appreciate how much the Churches share in common. Many will disagree with his opinions, but no-one should doubt the weight of the scholarship that informed them.

a. *Towards the Setting*

At seventy-three years of age, Green was too old to change his opinions, but he used these years in the late thirties to re-affirm the truths in which he had always believed and the clarity of his teaching is remarkable. Throughout 1936, in spite of his other commitments, Green was busily engaged in his work on the *Setting of the Constitution of the Church in Wales*. His general Visitation charge to his diocese in that year contained words that were soon to become familiar to all readers of his book when it was published a year later.

In his Visitation charge, Green described the respective functions of the incumbent and the churchwardens within a parish. What he said about their respective functions may now be read in chapter nine of the *Setting*. Both the incumbent and the churchwardens were men under authority, the authority of the bishop "in accordance with the Constitution, canons and regulations of the Church in Wales".

"The incumbent" said Green, "is not responsible to the church-wardens, nor to the parochial church council, nor to any except the bishop and the archdeacons, for the manner in which he performs his duties". At the same time the churchwarden's office was an ancient one to which many duties had become attached down the ages and to which great importance still belonged.

Although it revealed a weight of learning, Green's exposition was not purely academic but served a pastoral purpose, and to that extent Green was never a true academic. If priest and people understood their duties more clearly, the Ministry of the whole Church would be more effective. It was good for incumbents and churchwardens to know how they stood in the constitution of the Church, but there was a note of warning; "It would very very unwise for clergy or laity to overemphasise their legal rights. As far as possible, your rights should be remembered only at the back of your mind". This was sensible advice comparable to Green's statement to a previous conference that the electoral roll of a parish was so important that the Constitution could be improved by ordering the roll to be scrapped in every third year, a proposal more radical than the recent provision for renewing the roll every five years.

Green's only major printed work, *The Setting of the Constitution of the Church in Wales*, was published on Ascension Day, 6th May, 1937, as he was preparing to attend the Coronation of King George VI. At his own expense, Green generously gave a presentation copy to every member of the Governing Body and the Representative Body of the Church in Wales as well as to the staff of those bodies. On 7th June, 1937 Viscount Sankey wrote to thank Green for his own presentation copy of the *Setting*. He said that he thought the book was excellent and he wished that he had been able to write it himself. He still had his original drafts of his work on the Constitution but Green's book had made him feel rather nervous, because had he realised "there was such a mass of learning behind it and that there was a man who knew it all, I am afraid I should have feared to rush in". The *Western Mail* hailed the book as having said everything that could possibly be worth saying about the Church in Wales, but it was not reviewed in the learned journals. Whether this omission was caused by the paucity of canon lawyers who could estimate its worth or by the lack of interest among medieval historians because its subject was too modern, we shall never know. A short notice in the *Law Quarterly Review* in 1938 did not know what to make of the book although Green had received the degrees of B.C.L. and D.C.L. from his *alma mater* for his work. The book seems to have been beyond the purview of modern historians and the official history of the Church in Wales does not even mention it.

A formal resolution of thanks to Green for his book and for the complimentary copies was proposed by Sankey and seconded by Sir John Bankes at the meeting of the Governing Body on the 29th September. In thanking the Governing Body for its resolution, Green expressed the hope that his book would help "Churchmen in Wales particularly those younger than himself".

b. *The Setting*

"There are two kinds of fools: one says, This is old, therefore it is good; the other says, This is new, therefore it is better" -Dean Inge.

Green's book was a great comfort to Churchpeople in Wales, not least because there was in Sankey's words "a man who knew it all" and had been prepared to devote time and scholarship to interpret the Constitution not only for posterity but also to reassure many who had lived through the trauma of disestablishment that while they may have lost much that they took for granted in their lives as Anglicans, they still possessed the essential Catholic heritage intact. Although severed from the Church of England, they were still part of a province of the world-wide Anglican communion of which the Archbishop of Canterbury was the head.

Few Welsh Churchpeople to-day would want to undo the disestablishment that was forced upon the Church in Wales in 1920. By 1937 Green had realised that uncovenanted blessings had accrued to the Church in Wales through disestablishment in spite of the Church's original opposition. Disestablishment enabled the Church in Wales to be more closely identified with the Welsh people and the Church's position in Wales was strengthened. The key to the *Setting*, as of the Constitution itself is episcopacy. The word was almost Green's middle name even before he became a bishop. What kind of episcopacy did Green proclaim? Certainly not any kind of episcopal system which threw up bishops from the ranks beneath in a manner analogous to the Lutherans or the American Methodists or Frederick of Prussia's proposals for the Anglican bishopric in Jerusalem in 1841. As Canon E.T. Davies has described in his popular layman's guide to the Constitution, episcopacy for Green, and therefore for the Church in Wales, was not simply the salt on the egg without which one's breakfast is less enjoyable but it should rather be regarded as the yeast without which you cannot bake bread. Episcopacy was that without which there was no Church at all. *Ubi episcopus; ibi ecclesia.*

Such was Green's view, a view that went beyond what might be called constitutional episcopacy or even the essentials of the Lambeth Quadrilateral of 1888 with its insistence upon the historic episcopate as an essential in a reunited Christian Church. Certainly when Archbishop Fisher of Canterbury appealed to the Free Churches to take episcopacy into their system in 1945, he did not imagine that they would be adopting Green's model of the monarchical bishop.

The address 'Lord Bishop' as a title of courtesy for such a monarchical bishop had nothing to do with membership of the House of Lords in Green's view but is "older than the Crown and Parliament of England". Thus Green disposed of the argument that the bishops of the Church in Wales had been deprived of their titles of courtesy by disestablishment. Nor for that matter, did the Constitution confer "any authority or power upon the bishops which did not already belong to them by Divine Commission" because "the Church is a theocracy, not a democracy".

At the same time, Green admitted that history teaches us that the bishops "did normally consult their presbyters and in varying modes co-operate with the laity". Thus the Constitution is the result of consultation and co-operation between the Welsh bishops and their clergy and laity. It is a solemn covenant or concordat between them.

Yet ecclesiastical law alone regulates the bishop's exercise of his ministry. The totality of the Christian Ministry stands in the bishop alone. All subordinate ministries are summed up in his own and some ministrations such as the consecration of other bishops or the ordination, institution or collation of clergymen to benefices, are peculiar to the order of bishops. Officers in the diocese such as chancellors, archdeacons, rural deans or churchwardens derive their authority from the bishop as does every parochial worker who is appointed indirectly by the incumbent. Priests are admitted to the order of bishops by being raised up from above through those who are already bishops and not by the act of a democratic assembly pushing them up from below.

A further chapter of Green's book is devoted to the method of appointing bishops. Bishops in the Church in Wales are appointed by an electoral college that consists of the Archbishop and the diocesan bishops of the province; six clerical and six lay electors from the vacant diocese and three clerical and three lay electors from each of the other dioceses. Green commended this system because a bishop was not being elected for his own diocese alone but for the whole province and for the good of the Church at large. When the bishop-elect has been confirmed as bishop by the diocesan bishops in synod, then he may proceed to administer his diocese and to make all necessary appointments, but he cannot consecrate other bishops nor ordain nor confirm the baptised until he himself has been consecrated by his fellow bishops. After his consecration, the new bishop is enthroned in his own cathedral.

In subsequent chapters Green wrote of the subordinate ministries and the qualifications required for Holy Orders as well as the disqualifications that he elicited from his manuals of medieval canon law. Was Green being ingenious or ingenuous in failing to acknowledge the historical accident by which this medieval canon law had survived the vicissitudes of the Reformation? In 1543 commissioners had been appointed to compile a new code of ecclesiastical law, and that code had been revised by Archbishop Cranmer, but politics impeded the progess of the work. When the appointment of the commissioners was renewed in 1550, their progress was checked by the accession of Queen Mary. The *Reformatio Legum Ecclesiasticarum* of 1571 was a code of post-Reformation canons that were supposed to supersede the medieval *Corpus Iuris Canonici* as well as the provincial constitutions, but the reform had no official approval. That meant that the medieval canon law continued in use in the Church of England provided that it was not contrary to the limits specified in the Act for the Submission of the Clergy of 1534. It is an irony of history that the failure of Cranmer and the Reformers to produce an alternative code of ecclesiastical law because "neither the nobles the gentry nor the people had any desire to see the re-establishment of ecclesiastical discipline"[16] made it possible for Charles Green to invoke the *Corpus Iuris Canonici* in defence of the Constitution of the Church in Wales four hundred years later, as if the Reformation had never taken place at all.

Green returns to a general discussion of ecclesiastical law and its contribution to the Church in Wales in chapter five. He admitted that the Church in Wales was not "irrevocably tied to that legal system, as it existed then" (on 30th March, 1920, the date of disestablishment) but it could be revised or altered through the Governing Body where the laity and clergy "share with the provincial synod of bishops the duty of forming and enacting ecclesiastical canons and laws".

The laity, the people of God, is the subject of chapter four. One is admitted to the laity by Baptism and Confirmation and therefore every qualified elector of the Church in Wales must have been baptised and confirmed. Green follows this with a study of Christian initiation and the instruction that is given to neophytes before they are confirmed in order to become regular communicants.

In chapter six Green returns to the bishop and his functions as the sole source of mission and jurisdiction in the diocese as well as his oversight as chief pastor and his power of Order. Chapter seven describes the Councils of the diocese, the diocesan synod and the cathedral chapter. New schemes for all the cathedrals of the Church in Wales were authorised by the Governing Body between March 1921 and 2nd October, 1930, when the scheme was passed for Monmouth. In this chapter Green goes on to describe the function of the rural deanery chapter of clergy and the diocesan conference "in all respects subject to the Governing body of the Church in Wales", and the ruridecanal conference, which consists of lay representatives from each parish of the rural deanery and the licensed readers together with the clergymen of the deanery.

The officers of the bishop and his courts are described in chapter eight together with the functions of the Archdeacon's court, the Vicar General and the Chancellor, the commissary and the Registrar, the rural dean and the churchwardens, whose functions are more fully discussed in chapter nine which deals with the parish. The incumbent who "alone has the cure of souls within its bounds" is hailed as the "distinguishing mark of a real parish". Green explains the origins of the titles rector, vicar, curate and perpetual curate and relates the incumbent's authority to that of the bishop. The office and duties of churchwardens are described together with the task of the parochial authority in compiling and revising the electoral roll; the vestry meeting; the parochial church council and the minor officers of the parish such as the parish clerk, where one existed.

In the Church in Wales, the bishops under the presidency of the Metropolitan form the ancient provincial synod, but they do not exercise judicial and legislative powers in the synod, but only through the Governing Body. These councils of the province are described in chapter ten with a further reminder that the rights of the Governing Body are devolved from above and not conferred from beneath and that the Archbishop and diocesan bishops sit and act "as representing the ancient provincial synod" as an order separate both from the clergy and the laity. The Archbishop of Wales is the president of the Governing Body. Legislative procedure in the Governing body is by bill procedure and a bill must be passed by a majority of two-thirds of the members present and voting in each of the three orders before the president promulgates it as a canon of the Church in Wales and binding on all its members. The constitution gives the widest possible powers to the Governing Body.

The final chapters of the *Setting* deal with the Archbishop as Metropolitan of Wales, the method of his election and the tenure of his office; the appointment of the Archbishop's Registrar and the courts of the province; the functions of the Representative Body; the responsibility for consecrated places and things and the part that the diocesan board of finance must play in raising the annual diocesan Quota for the central funds of the Church in Wales and in providing money every year for the general purposes of the diocese. Under the heading of subjunctive associations, Green dealt with the relationship between the Church and human institutions such as the family, the state and religious communities, schools and colleges, parochial organisations whose constitution "has been approved and placed in a schedule by the diocesan conference".

In his penultimate chapter, Green demonstrated how the constitution affects the Christian life of the Church and of its individual members. "Neither individualism nor anarchy" he claimed "are compatible with membership of the Church". In the sphere of conduct, Green asserted that a high standard is set before the Church. Under the direction of the first Apostles, the public discipline of the Church originated and so the Governing Body provides for the trial of any member of the Church in Wales for criminal or immoral or scandalous behaviour, but it is typical of Green's unrealistic approach to this area of ecclesiastical jurisdiction that he regretted the omission of the charge of drunkenness from the scheme for the discipline of Church members. The picture of hundreds of communicants who had been found guilty of drunkenness in the magistrates' courts, appearing before the provincial court of the Church in Wales to be tried again, belongs so much to the middle ages that it can only be laughed out of court in the twentieth century. At the same time Green's general observation is valid, that the "scheme is a witness to the standard which is expected of all members of the Christian Church".

In his desire for the restoration of godly discipline, Green was close to the ideals of the Puritans, but in another respect he had departed far from the Puritan prohibition of everything that is not commanded in the Bible. That was in the public worship of the Church where Green noted that the ceremonies were not necessarily prohibited simply because they were not prescribed in the rubrics. His last-but-one chapter gave Green the opportunity to comment upon the power of the Governing Body to alter the rites, ceremonies and formularies of the Church by bill procedure. Since hymns and organs are permitted in the worship of the Church although they are not ordered to be used, so also may censers for the burning of incense be used because they accompany what has to be said and done.

The final chapter of Green's *magnum opus* concerns the relationship between the Church and the State. Green recognised "a fundamental dissonance between the Christian Church and the State for their aims and processes differ". Provided that they made no claim to coercive jurisdiction, the state allowed the Church to have its own courts. The state no longer recognised the ecclesiastical law as part of the law of the land, but if decisions of the church courts were rejected, the state provided a legal remedy where there had been breaches of the fictitious contract that bound together members of the Church in Wales. In her constitution the Church in Wales had the power to alter and modify the ecclesiastical law as embodied in any Act of Parliament by declaring, for example, that the "Public Worship Regulation Act of 1874 and the decisions of the English Courts or of the Judicial Committee of the Privy Council, in relation to discipline and ceremonial, do not form part of the ecclesiastical law of the Church in Wales", as Green had reminded Hensley Henson in 1922. The Church's title to its property is secured by its transference to the Representative Body through the Welsh Church Acts. The Churches and churchyards are protected. In Green's opinion, the clergy of the Church in Wales still enjoyed their former civil privileges and protection. In the matter of marriages in the churches of the Church in Wales, the state continued to protect the Church and to confirm her acts as if disestablishment had not occurred. The state allowed the Church to hold the ancient churchyards that had been closed by order in Council before disestablishment and the churchyards that were considered to be private benefactions after 1662 as well as the churchyards that had been acquired since disestablishment. By the end of 1936 only 146 out of a possible 819 transferable churchyards had been taken over by the local authorities concerned who were obviously not anxious to add the burden of churchyard maintenance to their annual budget.

Green ended his book with the words, in Latin, that Jesus spoke to the Pharisees and the Herodians when they tried to trap him with the question about paying taxes to Caesar: Reddite quae sunt Caesaris, Caesari: Quae sunt Dei, deo (St. Mark xii, 17). The Latin is appropriate for one whose mind was essentially that of a medieval canon lawyer and Our Lord's enigmatic reply is perhaps a fitting conclusion to a book by a man whose erastianism was finaly overcome by his triumphalism.

Modern minds who confront Green through his *Setting of the Constitution* often accuse him of being not only high-minded but also high-handed. The book is concerned with Church law and administration and is not intended to be a manual of pastoral care. It is in fact a pioneer in its own field and Green was not afraid of the mistakes that he might be making. He had hoped that others might follow him into the field, but few if any did. The loss that this shortage of ecclesiastical lawyers would be for the future Church was still on his mind when he addressed his diocesan conference at Machynlleth on 29th August, 1939 and noted with regret the demolition of the building in London known as "Doctors Commons".

Doctors Commons was an association of ecclesiastical lawyers which had its headquarters near St. Paul's Cathedral from 1565 until 1857 and from which the judges who practised in the Archbishops' courts had been taken. Green observed that this body of men had never been dissolved by statute although Doctors Commons had effectively been dissolved by the Court of Probate Act in 1857.

It was not simply from antiquarian taste that Green regretted the passing of Doctors Commons with their magnificent library but because he saw the need for a similar institution in Wales which might provide judges for the Church courts. With the demise of Doctors Commons Green believed that the Church had lost amazing learning and the sympathetic understanding of Church history and polity that had been found there. As a result the Church's administration was conducted by men who were amateurs in ecclesiastical affairs. The matter was more urgent for Wales because of her special constitution, thought Green, and he seriously wondered whether a miniature Doctors Commons could not be set up in Wales with a library and lecture room at which studies in ecclesiastical law could be pursued under the direction of a board that had been nominated, of course, by the Governing Body. From the students at such an institution, future archbishops might select "Advocates and proctors of the Church in Wales".

It is a piece of nineteenth century fantasy that would have given Gilbert and Sullivan a field-day. Green was flying a kite. His vision of a Doctors Commons in the Church in Wales was nothing more than the dream of an old man in his seventy-sixth year. The dream has its more frightening aspect which becomes the nightmare of ecclesiastical courts constantly in session with an army of litigants and a procession of advocates and witnesses. The stream of ecclesiastical anathemas, censures and Archbishop's judgements might have provided a medievalist's paradise but they would have had as much relationship to the realities of the twentieth century as the bow and arrow did to the hydrogen bomb.

In that analogy lies the uncomfortable suggestion that sooner or later what is stored up for security will be used in self-defence. They who take the sword will perish by it. So too, they who seek their security in ecclesiastical law will lose their spiritual credibility by litigation.

c. *The Macnaghten Case*

The issues in dispute between Alfred Edwin Monahan, Vicar, archdeacon and later Bishop of Monmouth and Edmund Loftus Macnaghten, Vicar of St. Thomas-over-Monnow, Monmouth, did not really concern Charles Green but the case is worth describing because it illustrates the weakness of legalism and litigation and Charles Green involved himself in it as Archbishop and he presided over the provincial court that heard the appeal from Macnaghten's widow in December 1942.

It will be recalled that Green was careful to remind Church Officers that they would be foolish to force their rights upon other Christians in a legalistic way. The dispute between Monahan and Macnaghten could have been thus avoided and could best be described as one of psychological or personality conflicts. The issues were trivial by the standards of any court.

Edmund Loftus Macnaghten, born in 1879, had taken his degree at Trinity College Dublin in 1902 and prepared for ordination at Ely Theological College. After a chequered career for part of which he had practised as an osteopath in Harley Street, he became Vicar of St. Thomas-over-Monnow in 1939 through the influence of his friend Alfred Edwin Monahan. Monahan had taken his degree at Trinity College Dublin in 1903 although he was two years older than Macnaghten, and he had also proceeded to Ely Theological College. He became Vicar of Monmouth in 1912 and archdeacon in 1930.

No sooner had Monahan installed Macnaghten in the neighbouring parish to his own than the two men began to quarrel. The extant correspondence is unedifying to say the least, but it appears that Macnaghten resented Monahan's official authority as archdeacon and Monahan was determined to keep Macnaghten in his place. Most of the difficulty was caused because Macnaghten presumed upon Monahan's friendship and then resented Monahan's lofty reaction. So Macnaghten absented himself from Archdeacon

Monahan's court without permission and he replied to Monahan's strongly-worded letter of disapproval of 9th May, 1939 in the following terms on the next day:

"My dear Archdeacon,

Just fancy you writing such a "fierce" letter to the old Priest, who had no intention whatever of "affronting" you! I simply did not know that my presence was required further. Please forgive me. We are looking forward to seeing you and the family to-morrow.

Yours as ever,
E.L. Macnaghten".

When this approach by Macnaghten was rebuffed by Monahan, Macnaghten resorted to angry letters. He tried to stand on the dignity of his parochial rights as incumbent of Overmonnow and he told Monahan on 21st August, 1939:

". . .in the future neither of your assistant curates is to teach in the Overmonnow Church Day Schools until the consent of the Parish Priest has been obtained".

On 10th April, 1940, Macnaghten wrote to Monahan in the following terms:

"The Revd Dr. E.L. Macnaghten presents his compliments to the Ven. the Archdeacon of Monmouth and states that he will not be present at the Visitation on April 11th. Dr. Macnaghten is ill-a condition aggravated by the conduct of the Archdeacon; which is an insult to the Priestly Order, an outrage on the Christian Fellowship and utterly beneath contempt".

Thus in a lunatic flash of inspiration Macnaghten summarised the whole sad procedure with which he has become associated. Macnaghten was ill, more ill than he realised, and Monahan's conduct was beneath contempt.

As if in response to some atavistic Irish feud, Monahan continued to challenge Macnaghten. In August 1940, Monahan became Bishop of Monmouth and he appointed Samuel Morris Davies as Archdeacon of Monmouth. Through his archdeacon, Monahan vicariously continued to provoke Macnaghten. On 15th March, 1941, Archdeacon Davies wrote to ask Macnaghten if he could pay an official visit to St. Thomas-over-Monnow at 2.30 p.m. on Friday March 21st so that he could get to know Macnaghten and his churchwardens. On 18th March, 1941, Macnaghten replied that he would welcome Davies as a brother priest and he invited him to lunch, but he was opposed to an official visit because "Our Blessed Lord has told me that officialism is a great curse in the Church, is robbing her of spirituality and power, is a weapon of Satan causing grievous loss to souls and is most saddening to the Sacred Heart".

Archdeacon Davies replied that he would not be visiting Macnaghten as a brother priest but in his official capacity as Archdeacon of Monmouth. On 22nd March, 1941, Macnaghten replied that he did not wish to meet Davies as an official. On 18th June, 1941, Macnaghten received an official citation from the Archdeacon's Registrar to an archdeacon's visitation in St. Thomas-over-Monnow. Macnaghten excused himself from attending because he had a bad heart, but he added: "I do not admit the right of any Priest to speak in this Church without my consent". The Archdeacon postponed the visitation to 10th July.

Macnaghten replied by post-card on 4th July. He forbade any priest from conducting a service or speaking in St. Thomas's church without his consent and announced that he would not be in church for the visitation "and the doors may be locked to prevent what is regarded as a contemplated outrage".

The doors were locked, and when Macnaghten realised that he might have gone too far in preventing an archdeacon from carrying out a legitimate duty, he started to object that he was not being correctly addressed in official correspondence from the diocese of Monmouth as "the Rev. *Doctor* E.L. Macnaghten as courtesy requires".

On 15th September 1941, Macnaghten wrote to Monahan in hysterical terms describing what had happened as the work of anti-Christ and calling upon Monahan "to repent, confess, amend". On 20th September a note from Macnaghten was delivered to Monahan while he was conducting an Ordination Service in St. Mary's Monmouth just before the Gospel. Macnaghten claimed that his wife was very ill and that he was in great anguish of mind. He asked Monahan to visit him for a few minutes while he was in Monmouth, but Monahan declined and agreed to see him at Bishopstow by appointment.

On 27th November 1941, under the presidency of Sir John Eldon Bankes, the provincial court of the Church in Wales met at the Tredegar Estate Offices in Newport to hear the case of the Bishop of Monmouth v. the Revd Dr. Edmund Loftus Macnaghten, Vicar of St. Thomas-over-Monnow. The four members of the court under Bankes' presidency were all reasonable and kindly men. They were, Bishop Havard of St. Asaph; Canon B.C. Edwards, Rector of Tenby; Revd J. Gwyn Davies, Vicar of Sketty and a future dean of Monmouth, and Judge Frank Davies. The proceedings of the court demonstrated that the real conflict was between Monahan and Macnaghten and had nothing to do with Archdeacon S.M. Davies.

When Macnaghten was being questioned about his early departure from a visitation that Archdeacon Monahan had conducted in 1939, he admitted that he did go out before the visitation had been completed. Under cross-examination from Mr. St. John G. Micklethwait, K.C., Macnaghten described Monahan's visitation as: "fifty-three minutes of the most awful bilge I have ever heard from anyone. The archdeacon talked the most awful rubbish about finances. A schoolboy of ten would have got the cane for it". Asked about the letter of 15th March, 1941 from Archdeacon Davies, Macnaghten said that he realised that it was a letter from the archdeacon, but he claimed that he was not very familiar with the position of an archdeacon because "I had been practising as a doctor in London for seventeen years, and I was not in touch with these things".

The court found Macnaghten guilty of only one of the three charges that were brought against him by the Bishop of Monmouth, that of conduct giving just cause for scandal or offence under section 27, 5(g) of chapter eleven of the constitution. In the opinion of the court Macnaghten's offence was "not a grave one" and the president thought that Macnaghten was under a misconception of what the archdeacon proposed to do in an apparently sincere belief that the archdeacon was exceeding his powers. Macnaghten had expressed his willingness to apologise to Archdeacon Davies in a letter written before the legal petition was served and he had tendered a full apology both to the bishop and to the archdeacon after the petition had been served on him. He was found not guilty of violating his ordination vows, but Monahan deprived him of his living and inhibited him from ever officiating in the diocese of Monmouth again. The mandate of deprivation and the notice of inhibition were published in full in the *South Wales Argus* and the *Monmouthshire Beacon*.

In September 1942 Macnaghten filed a petition alleging that Monahan was "actuated by malice, personal ill-will and animosity; that the bishop had uttered defamatory statements of him, that the bishop had been guilty of violation of his consecration vows, had passed an unlawful sentence upon him and that the bishop's action in passing the maximum sentence had caused grave scandal." Macnaghten died before the date appointed for the hearing of the petition but his widow was allowed to proceed with it.

The provincial court sat to hear the case of Mrs. Ethel May Macnaghten v. the Bishop of Monmouth on 22nd and 23rd December, 1942. Archbishop Green presided and judgement was given in favour of Bishop Monahan on Wednesday 6th January, 1943. The judgement of the provincial court was read out by Archbishop Green from behind a small oak gate-legged table at the foot of the chancel steps in the parish church of St. John the Baptist, Cardiff, while the bishops of Llandaff, St. David's, St. Asaph and Swansea and Brecon sat around the table with the registrar of the provincial court, Mr. L.S. Whitehead. The judgement, on eleven foolscap pages, concluded that the petitioner had failed to substantiate the charges made in the petition. The Bishop in doing what he did, was not actuated by malice, personal ill-will or animosity. He did not utter any defamatory statements about Macnaghten. He did not violate his consecration vows nor did his conduct cause any scandal. The court accepted the bishop's assertion that he would have taken the same course if his own brother had written the letters which Mr. Macnaghten had written to the archdeacon and had locked the door against him.

The case has been described so fully to be fair to all the parties concerned. It brought credit to no-one and in retrospect it can only be regretted. It killed Macnaghten, foolish and misguided though he was, and it revealed Monahan in a most unfortunate light. It brought out the least attractive aspect of Green's character, his desire to play the ecclesiastical judge.

d. After the setting

What could follow the *Setting of the Constitution* but Green's own eclipse? Green had prepared for the book for such a long time. Two years before its publication he had read the first chapter on the Historic Episcopate to the Monmouth Clerical Association. Green delivered the same chapter as an address to the Swansea and Brecon diocesan conference on 13th September, 1935 in support of the Archbishop of Canterbury's deprecation of "language which would ground Episcopacy merely on the opinion that it is perhaps the wisest and most efficient form of Church order".

In a similar way Green addressed the Llandaff diocesan conference on 17th October, 1935. He was continuing the policy started by Archbishop Edwards of visiting every diocese in the province during his first year as archbishop. But he would not comment upon the economic and industrial problems of the Diocese of Llandaff at that time. He turned instead to "some aspects of the ecclesiastical background of the Constitution of the Church in Wales" as an antidote to what he regarded as the mental obsession with economic ills.

It was at this stage in his life that Green began to be obsessed with his own physical ills. His first bout of illness had come in April 1935 and it was then that he granted a commission to Bishop Wentworth Shields to act as assistant bishop in the Diocese of Bangor. Green was ill again during August 1936 although he continued to work on his book while he was still in bed. His poor state of health brought on an attack of shingles at the end of August and he spent most of September convalescing in the Lake District.

At the end of May 1937 Green received the news of his brother Wilfrith's death at Beaconsfield where he had retired from the army with the rank of Brigadier-General in 1928. Eight years younger than Charles, Wilfrith was Green's youngest surviving brother and his death left only Charles and Kenneth and their two sisters Elswith and Edith. At the end of September 1937, Green and his wife went to Llandaff to meet the dean, D.J. Jones, to select a site for their own grave. The same careful preparations that had been made for their marriage nearly forty years earlier were now being made for their deaths. In September 1937 Green shared the government's ignorance of the extent to which international events would overtake their meticulous preparations.

Green could never have guessed what the condition of Llandaff Cathedral would be when the day of his death arrived. He believed in the policy of appeasement and only ten days before Neville Chamberlain returned from Munich in September 1938 waving his piece of paper, Green told the Bangor diocesan conference how much the speech of the Chancellor of the Exchequer, Sir John Simon, on 15th July agreed with what Christians had been saying during the last twenty years and longer. Simon had pointed to the "folly of the world's fantastic expenditure upon armaments" and the menace that this held for the future "unless the arms race can be halted by international appeasement". Green went on to remind the conference of the wise words that he himself had used in a sermon before the University of Oxford in 1928 about the great evil of war, and he said that it was a Christian duty "to urge. . .that warfare essentially belongs to a lower stage in the process of evolution-that a bellicose spirit is not consistent with the ideal which we seek to realise". At the same time Green believed in being realistic about the preparations that should be made in the event of any war occurring and he commended the work of the Red Cross to the conference in 1938 as a means of knowing what should be done in the event of "the horrors of warfare from the air". Green asked the clergy and leading laity to attend instruction classes in the air-raid precaution services.

Green spent the second part of March 1939 ill in bed with more serious kidney trouble which required x-rays and intensive treatment although he had no operation. Bishop Wentworth Sheilds carried out Green's ordination service at Bangor Cathedral on 24th June while Green was in Scotland recovering from his illness, but he broke his holiday to attend the electoral college at Llandaff which elected Bishop John Morgan of Swansea and Brecon to the see of Llandaff on 22nd June. The premature death of his friend Timothy Rees after only a short episcopate at Llandaff had saddened Green, but he was satisfied with the election of his protegé John Morgan as Timothy Rees's successor.

Another old friend, Canon H.R. Johnson died in retirement at Ryde, Isle of Wight, on 25th January, 1940. Green himself was taken ill on Tuesday 9th April with heart trouble and low blood pressure, an illness from which he suffered for four months during which he needed the constant attention of a nurse who lived at Bishopscourt. Between April and July he was too ill even to record the usual daily items in his diary, but he managed to collate to the deanery of Bangor and to the archdeaconry of Merioneth on 1st July, and he was well enough to preside at the electoral college in Bangor Cathedral which elected A.E. Monahan as the third Bishop of Monmouth on 7th August, 1940.

Archbishop Green's duty of presiding over the meetings of the Governing Body was severely limited because of the war. After the meeting of 27th September, 1939, the work of the Governing Body was entrusted to the war committee which had no power to deal with any matter that required Bill procedure, but it met twice in 1940, three times in 1941 and three times before 2nd October, 1942, when Green decided to assess the situation at a special meeting of the Governing Body in the Temple of Peace in Cardiff.

The presidential address on that occasion was short. Green paid tribute to the memory of his friend Gilbert Cunningham Joyce who had died shortly after retiring from the bishopric of Monmouth. Frank Morgan, Timothy Rees, H.R. Johnson and Gilbert Joyce, so many of Green's old friends were departing. But Green still thought that the Church's first duty was "to convert the people to faith in Christ". Only when we loved God, he said, should we be capable of loving our neighbour as ourselves. He concluded his short address by urging the Governing Body to take care that their committees consisted only of members of the Governing Body.

Green's heart trouble that had caused him to have at least one stroke by this time, had also slowed him down. He tended to prepare everything even further ahead than usual so that he could be sure to have everything ready in good time. Thus his Easter sermon for Bangor Cathedral was prepared at the beginning of February but he was taken ill with bronchitis on Maundy Thursday and he had to be out of action for the first fortnight in April. His sermon was read for him by someone else but it could have caused the reader no difficulty because it was most carefully written out in Green's firm and clear handwriting.

In that sermon, one of his last in Bangor Cathedral, Green returned to his beloved theme of Christian education in its fulness. He reflected that modern education was largely scientific, "that is based on the evidence of material facts, what can be measured, weighed and calculated". Mechanics and Engineering, he admitted "are attractive ... but when we come to the realm of Art, to the study of the whole personality of man, and to the discipline of human conduct, we find ourselves at sea, as the saying runs, unless we have learned to commune with God through the risen Christ. For the complete satisfaction of man, something more is needed than science and mechanics".

Green had sufficiently recovered by the end of April to begin the last of his triennial visitations of his diocese which he completed on 16th May, 1942 after twelve sessions in various centres throughout the diocese. Green's last visitation charge as a bishop was fairly short and was concerned with several practical matters in the midst of the war, such as the written reports of army, navy or air-force settlements in their parishes that he had requested from the clergy together with an account of how the clergy were providing for the moral and spiritual needs of the service-men in their settlements. Green also wanted to know how much money had been contributed by the parishes to the Lord Mayor's Empire Air Raid Distress fund. He went on to draw attention to complaints about the state of Church burial-grounds, and he appealed for greater support for the widows and orphans of deceased clergymen.

In speaking of the war, Green discounted the pacifist stance in the face of "material evils" which he believed could only be fought with "material weapons". He thought that prevention of the evil would have been better and every effort should be made to enlighten the public mind "when the day of peace comes". Man's greatest need, concluded Green, was for communion with God through meditation and prayer, and he ended his final charge with the familiar words of Tennyson's *Morte d'Arthur*, "More things are wrought by prayer than this world dreams of".

Green was ill again with heart trouble at the end of October and he had to be attended by his doctor until December. While he was ill, he continued to read Pascal, a frequent favourite with Green, although he has recorded nothing of the impression that Pascal made upon him. On 19th December he ordained two priests and a deacon in Bangor Cathedral and he presided over the special provincial court in Cardiff for the trial of "Macnaghten v. the Bishop of Monmouth" on 22nd and 23rd December. On 27th December Green was again confined to his bed.

The need to give written expression to the provincial court's judgement in the case of Mrs. Macnaghten v. Monahan, brought Green out of bed on 28th December. He completed the draft of a sentence that could be delivered as the judgement of the court but his draft was not used because the judgement was better drafted by Mr. Justice Lewis.

If Green was feeling his age and admitting that others could draft legal sentences better than he, he must have marvelled at the longevity of the old ecclesiastical hierarchy in Bangor. Griffith Roberts, appointed dean in 1903, had welcomed Green to the diocese in 1928 and died in 1943 in his ninety-eighth year. Green attended his funeral on 10th February. Bishop Watkin Herbert Williams who had appointed Dean Roberts and resigned the see in 1925, celebrated his ninety-eighth birthday in 1943 with "affectionate greetings and their congratulations" from the Governing Body meeting in September 1943, the last over which Green presided.

Green's address to the Governing Body on 29th April, 1943 was printed in full in the minutes at the request of the members because of its importance. His tone was optimistic. Green reminded his listeners that material reforms would never bring lasting happiness without the presence of Christ in their lives. He went on to speak of the need to maintain the Christian ministry in every parish and for the Church to be concerned about the proper supply and training of candidates for the ministry. Green said that the funds of the Representative Body were inadequate for the needs of the future especially if money depreciated after the war. Members of the Church would have to make larger financial contributions in the future. Green appealed to Churchpeople to give more during their lifetimes and to leave a legacy by their wills.

Green regretted the tendency to regard the Representative Body as an unlimited reservoir of funds, but he looked forward to the time when the Church in Wales would be able to afford to give a man in training for the ministry "two years" training in scientific theology" after an Arts degree and "finally a sixth year ... for the development of his devotional and homiletic gifts". He hoped that St. Michael's College in Llandaff would never cease to provide what was wanted for the three final years of this course and "there are rumours ... that generous benefactors will be ready, when the time arrives, to undo the disastrous results of the bombing which has sent the college to the west".

Within a few days of Green's death in the following May, an appreciation of Green's contribution to the foundation and development of the work of St. Michael's College appeared in the *Western Mail* from the pen of Glyn Simon then Warden of the college which had not yet returned from its war-time exile in St. David's. Glyn Simon had been Green's Warden of Ordinands and examining chaplain since 1931 until his appointment to St. Michael's in 1939. Simon owed a great deal to Green. In his tribute he recalled that others did too. It was Green who had been responsible for first bringing G.C. Joyce to Wales as sub-warden of St. Michael's College at Aberdare in 1892.

On Thursday 19th August, 1943, Charles Green celebrated his seventy-ninth birthday with a Laus Deo in red-ink in his diary. Was he thanking God that he had lived so long or thanking him that he was almost home? It was his last birthday.

Green managed to keep going through the winter. On January 6th, one year after delivering the judgement of the provincial court in Cardiff, he was at St. Fagan's with his wife for the funeral of her younger sister Gwendolen. By March the Bishop of Llandaff was taking his Confirmation services in Bangor. After a further spell in bed, Green came downstairs for lunch on Holy Saturday, 8th April, 1944 and sent his resignation of the Archbishopric of Wales to the Bishop of St. David's who was next in seniority among the bishops. Green sent a copy of his resignation to Mr. Whitehead, the Secretary of the Representative Body. Green resigned as Archbishop but remained as Bishop of Bangor and the old Adam hoped to stay long enough to influence the choice of his successor as Archbishop. In the event Green died before any decision had been taken about his successor as archbishop and the predictable appointment of the most senior bishop was made. The red-letter day that Green could not record in his diary but for which he was, as always, adequately prepared, came on the morning of Sunday 7th May, 1944. One month after he had resigned the archbishopric and one month before D-day, Charles Alfred Howell Green died peacefully at Bangor.

Green's body was taken from Bishopscourt to Llandaff Cathedral on Wednesday 10th May. Here Green had been ordained and here he had been installed as a canon and Archdeacon of Monmouth in 1914. Here he had been consecrated a bishop in 1921. The cathedral was barely recognisable as the place that he knew and loved. It had been badly damaged by enemy action in January 1941. His coffin was covered by a pall and surrounded by six candlesticks. It was placed before the altar in the lady chapel which was being used as the emergency cathedral. A vigil was kept there all night.

At 7.30 a.m. on Thursday the Dean celebrated a requiem and the Bishop of Llandaff celebrated at a Sung Requiem Eucharist at 11 a.m. The Burial service took place at 2 p.m. Green's wife and his youngest sister Edith were the chief mourners. His only surviving brother, Kenneth, was too ill to attend although his wife was present. Lady Merthyr and Mrs. Green's sister were also there. Many mourners had to stand outside and the visiting clergymen were not robed because of the lack of space. At Green's request they sang the Welsh hymn, *O Fryniau Caersalem*. The Bishop of Llandaff read the lessons and the Dean of Llandaff led the prayers. Bishop Prosser of St. David's read the words of committal as Green's body was lowered into the space in the churchyard that he had reserved in 1937 next to the nineteenth century deans Davey and Vaughan. In the meantime Bishop Timothy Rees had been buried in the grave next to Green. In February 1950 Green's grave was opened to receive the body of his wife who had lived with her sister, Mrs. de Winton at Brecon after Green's death. Memorial services for Green were held in Bangor Cathedral, St. Woolos Cathedral in Newport and at St. Elvan's Church, Aberdare at the same time as the funeral service was being conducted at Llandaff.

Green's obituary appeared in *The Times* on 8th May, 1944. It was written by his young friend Frederic Hood, the principal of Pusey House, Oxford, who later contributed the article on Green to the *Dictionary of National Biography*. Green had first met Frederic Hood when he made Freddie his examining chaplain in 1921 on the recommendation of Dr. Kidd, the warden of Keble. The main editorial in the *Western Mail* on the same day remarked upon the few distinctively Welsh characteristics that Green possessed although he was a "Welsh-speaking Welshman who had lived and laboured all his life in different parts of the Principality". The editorial accurately stated that Green tried to give light rather than heat in his sermons which "made their appeal to the mind, the judgement and faith based on a steadfast reasonableness, rather than emotion". Perhaps the editor was too shallow in his assessment of what constituted "distinctively Welsh characteristics". Green was not the product of the nineteenth century nonconformist subculture of the industrial areas that too often passes for genuine Welshness. There were Welsh influences upon his character from a more ancient rural background in west Wales. Green was certainly recognisable as a type of Welshman although he was very different in temperament from David Lloyd George whose contemporary he was. It should also be remembered that Green's father was English although he spent most of his ministry in Wales and had learned Welsh, and that all Green's secondary education as well as his higher education was received in England and it was the traditional classical education of a middle class gentleman in Victorian England. When Charles Green died, he belonged to a world that had passed away. He would have had little place in post-war Britain. He moved with poise in a world that he dominated with style. His leadership was beyond dispute and he transformed the Church in Wales because he was taller from the neck upwards, as Lloyd George would have said, than any other leader in the Church in Wales in his lifetime.

No one could ever doubt the clarity of his thinking. In matters of Historical scholarship he was not always correct, but that is to judge him by the harsh yardstick of the development in historical studies that has taken place since the war. In strict parlance, to parody his own words, he was not really a historian at all because he was not greatly concerned with the interpretation of historical records in their own setting. His was a lawyer's mind that sought evidence from the past to support his own arguments in the present. Historic continuity was his theme. He does not impress one as a profound theologian although he earned for himself a Doctorate in Divinity while he was still a busy parish priest. More than any other man he was the ecclesiastical administrative genius that the Church in Wales needed to cope with the reorganisation that was forced upon it by disestablishment. That he was also a liturgical scholar was a bonus that helped to stamp his style of Churchmanship indelibly upon the Church in Wales. Above all else Charles Green was a great Christian communicator and educator, perhaps the last of the Tractarians for what was his *Setting* but a Tract for the Times? Precisely what that meant is encapsulated in his address to his diocesan conference at Bangor on 22nd August, 1935, his first conference since he had become Archbishop of Wales. It was perhaps his finest hour. The following words from Green's speech form his most fitting epitaph:

"What is the purpose of sermons, speeches and books but to educate the communal mind? Education of a race or a nation is a tedious and lengthy process; but it is effective. It results in the birth of a generation which has assimilated the new principles, and will make them the standard and inspiration of its acts. When a man refuses to take part in the proclamation of an ideal on the ground that it is for the moment unattainable, he betrays his ignorance of the actual course of human history, he robs the generation to come of its hope of life. It is the privilege of the Christian Church to proclaim the message of love, humanity and peace. No member of the Church dare be silent. He must give voice openly and wholeheartedly for the ideals of his faith".

Notes

1. John Innes, *Old Llanelly* (Cardiff 1902) pp. 21, 22, 25, 110.
2. David W. James, *St. David's and Dewisland, A Social History* (U.W.P. 1981) pp. 140-145.
3. Herbert Hensley Henson, *Retrospect of an Unimportant Life* (3 vols. O.U.P. 1942-50) vol. 1 p. 11.
4. E.T. Davies, *Religion in the Industrial Revolution in South Wales* (U.W.P. 1965) p. 130.
5. *The Aberdare Times*, Sat. 2nd September, 1893.
6. Kenneth O. Morgan, *Rebirth of a Nation: Wales 1880-1980* (U.W.P. 1981) p. 440.
7. *South Wales Daily News*, 14th August, 1895.
8. *Merthyr Express*, Sat. 2nd June, 1894.
9. Eluned E. Owen, *The Later Life of Bishop Owen* (Llandysul 1961) pp. 265, 275.
10. *Ibid.* pp. 349, 367.
11. *The Times*, 17th, 19th, 21st and 23rd October, 1922.
12. Henson, *Retrospect*, vol 2, p. 277.
13. S.C. Carpenter, *Winnington-Ingram* (Hodder and Stoughton 1949) p. 156.
14. Owen Chadwick, *The Mind of the Oxford Movement* (Black, 1960) p. 33.
15. D. Parry-Jones, *A Welsh Country Parson* (Batsford 1975) p. 109.
16. Jasper Ridley, *Thomas Cranmer* (O.U.P. 1962) p. 331.